The Domination Game – Breaking Free

A Visionary Guide to the Rise of Cooperative Culture

by

Vyana Reynolds

ISBN: 979-8-9862748-6-7

DEDICATION

To the human race –

one family of fellow travelers on

our living blue planet we fondly call home.

CONTENTS

FROM THE AUTHOR

For millions of years, humans lived in symbiotic harmony with nature. Some ancient cultures still do. A few thousand years ago, the story changed, and humanity now faces an existential crisis and great suffering. Luckily, we know what got us into the pickle, and it is my view that it can get us out – the stories we tell about who we are and why we are here.

If we want to thrive on this planet as a species, we will need to reinvent ourselves. Humanity must transform our modern theme song from rugged individuals surviving in a dangerous world. In our current American culture, unbridled consumption takes the edge off our chronic experience of scarcity and isolation. So many Americans suffer from fear, mental illness, loneliness, and if the government didn't provide it, most of us wouldn't know how to grow food, create our own clean water, electricity or safely process our own waste.

We can either chose to live in a conscious community or an unconscious one.

Like about half of all Americans, I grew up in a "broken" home. My father left when I was three. Like a typical nuclear family, we were not part of a larger tribe of support, so when father left, I thought I had to fill his shoes and take care of myself and everyone else. I resentfully became an over responsible workaholic who judged anyone that didn't pull their weight. I thought "play" was a waste of time. I became an entrepreneur at age three to put food on the table. I taught my kindergarten class how to do long division because the teacher "wasn't doing her job" from my precocious 5-year-old perspective.

I've always wondered what it would have been like if I had actually experienced a childhood where "it takes a village to raise a child." This is especially rare now that it takes at least two jobs and two earners just to pay the basic bills of American household. That leaves no one to raise the children. I know of very few villages in America. As we continue to raise ourselves, we perpetuate the pattern of rugged individualism and the stories that fuel it.

The stories we write in our own minds during these formative years inform our perception of reality. We just assume "that's how it is." I know that I can easily get stuck in habits based on stories of the past. Some studies show that over 90% of the thoughts we think today are the same thoughts we had yesterday. Those thoughts will either deliver us or destroy us, so let's choose them wisely.

America is at a cross-roads as our political rhetoric coupled with the power of social media has succeeded in dividing us. We think the symptoms of society are the "problem" rather than the underlying assumptions we have forgotten to question. If we care about the continuation of our democracy, then we have the inescapable opportunity to heal our wounding. We must rewrite a unified story of our future – one that includes "life, liberty and the pursuit of happiness" for everyone.

If we are willing to do that work, we may remember our belonging within a community (or our role within an ecosystem). We may remember who and why we are here such that we become a regenerative culture -- one that values our relationships and connection, generosity in collaborative abundance, localized circular economics, caring for and listening to all living beings in a wholistic way, a world where humanity contributes to the ecosystem rather than depleting it. I believe we can create a culture where we spend more time asking better questions rather than defending our rigid opinions about how to merely treat symptoms.

This is not a utopian dream – but a new prerequisite to life on our home planet. The most powerful way we humans transform our thoughts, beliefs and ultimately our culture is by the stories we tell. We can predict the future based on our past performance or we can invent the future by redefining how we relate to one another.

This book is about waking up to the cultural norms that so many of us (including myself) have internalized as if it were human nature. In my experience, many of us have spent our lives either avoiding domination or trying to control others.

More than anything, humans want to be free and be in control of their own lives.

America's greatest legacy is the idea that we all deserve to be free. With freedom, however, comes responsibility for the impact we may have on each other and our home planet. We need to remember how we relate to one another and not just in the short run. Some indigenous cultures still remember this sacred relationship, and it is my hope that the rest of America will too, not because our survival depends on it, but because our spiritual amnesia is causing so much unnecessary suffering.

This book is not the "Truth." It represents my current "opinion" of who I believe myself to be having experienced my life through a particular lense. That lense has many labels that cannot capture the Truth of who I am, but may allow readers to better understand my limitations. Here is what you should know: I was raised in Tacoma, Washington, with a mother who valued education enough to make sure her four children got a "good one." We moved 11 times before I was 18, and father figures were scarce. She raised us in a Pentecostal Christian church, where my less than rigid beliefs made me feel like an imposter, all the while teaching Sunday School. I was raised to be straight, white, and an overachieving female. Luckily my mother was open minded and introduced me to the fairies who lived in the magical forests of the Pacific Northwest.

Money was scarce, so I learned to work early and work hard. My grandmother (of German descent) had advanced from welding ships during World War II to the first woman vice president of the local bank. My grandfather was a sheet metal worker. They were the only extended family that lived in relative proximity.

I connected with my father once a month growing up and was grateful for his deep spiritual adventurism. Raised by a Baptist minister, he carried a great deal of shame, and his suffering carved deep ravines in his brow as well as deep compassion for humanity. He offered healing on all levels as an old-school Osteopathic physician, homeopath and pioneer acupuncturist. He knew that most of human suffering was caused by the stories we told ourselves, and how the body tried to encourage us to evolve those views. The body never lied. He saw his job as getting his ego out of the way so that he could listen for the right question to ask the patient. He saw things wholistically and more deeply than anyone I knew.

After spending a year as a Rotary International exchange student in Istanbul, Turkey, I realized that America did to not have all the answers. My college years were spent studying various cultures and religions with a practical eye. I analyzed the end results of various belief systems and asked myself what made the most sense for humanity on a practical level. For example, I could see that the oppression of women did great harm (not just to women). It stunted humanity's evolution.

As an anthropology major, I was trained not to "judge" the culture I was observing, but to be a detached scientist. As someone who cared about humans, however, I had to point out the obvious. So, when it came time for me to choose a career, I chose the one that appeared to have the power to rewrite the rules of my culture. I chose to be a lawyer, to view the symptoms of my own culture wholistically, and listen for the questions that might heal us all – the questions that could evolve us collectively.

This book is an attempt to do just that. I offer it humbly knowing that my current viewpoint will "out" my own biases, unconscious prejudices, and that my views will evolve and change over time. My hope is that it may inspire others to do the same.

CHAPTER 1
THE INVISIBLE GAME WE'VE BEEN PLAYING

In America, we find ourselves deeply embedded in a game of domination masquerading as "democracy." A game with rules that most of us didn't write, unspoken assumptions that pretend to be truth, and carefully guarded hierarchies of power and wealth. Luckily, we are not victims. Rather, each of us continues to be complicit in perpetuating the game. When we internalize the rules as the norm by saying, "that's the way it has always been," we assume (incorrectly) that it is human nature to dominate others.

In this game, there are winners and losers, dominators and the dominated, those with power and those without. We embed it in unregulated capitalism that promotes competition at the expense of others. In other words, the game and the systematic structures that support it continues to be rigged by those who write the rules because certain dominating rulers initially framed our cultural paradigm.

This is what I call the Domination Game. It's a system so pervasive and normalized that we often don't even see it. But we all feel it. We feel it in the tightening of our shoulders at work, in the way we silence ourselves in uncomfortable conversations, in our instinct to either submit or resist. We feel it when we watch the endless stories of injustice on the news. The chronic anxiety it causes is baked into our institutions, economies, relationships, and even our inner dialogues. The result of the game, if continued, is a cycle of collective abuse. We inherited it, but we do not have to keep it.

This book is about waking up to that game, a culture based on domination, and choosing to play a different one. Why, because the price we ALL pay is much too high, personally and collectively. We are born into a game we didn't agree to play. Many of us have forgotten any other way to be and have come to the conclusion that domination is just our nature.

On a personal level, I listen to my inner tyrant tell me to lose weight and get "fit." I am not alone. This voice is heard by 95% of the women in America who are displeased with their current body shape. This voice was born from outer pressure created by a society that values lean and athletic bodies (a male prototype) that are not ideal for giving birth or breast feeding.

What if instead the ideal female form was ample enough to feed two, resistant to famine, round and voluptuous, designed for the potential of motherhood rather than stoic athletic competition? Ballerina bodies are revered in our culture because they pleased the male gaze in the French royal court hundreds of years ago. Today, ballerina's are so thin that some cannot menstruate. Don't get me started on how their feet suffer from their toe shoes! I'm not saying that women shouldn't aspire to attract males or that they are solely designed to carry babies (since I never chose to do that), but my natural body shape appears to be far more ample than male-dominated American culture appreciates.

Is it any wonder that so many of us are not choosing to have children? It's not considered sexy. Have you ever seen a magazine featuring pregnant women as the centerfold? Most of us are taught to fear pregnancy like the plague (at least until we are financial stable enough to afford the cost of having children in the modern era). I never met that criteria since I was always the breadwinner.

I made up a story of independence early in life when I decided never to rely on a man to support me financially. If I became dependent, I felt I would never be free to walk away if the domination game got out of hand, as it often does in America. Most women who are murdered in America are killed not by strangers, but by their husbands and male intimate partners. Intimate partner violence (IPV) is one of the leading causes of injury for women in the U.S. I value my freedom more than anything else, and most of my decisions around my relationships with men have centered around "avoiding domination" in a culture where husbands have traditionally had "the upper hand."

One of my survival methods to beat those statistics was to continue to be the "bread winner" in my marriages, so I was always free to walk away. The best thing I ever did to avoid domination was to take a self-defense class. Knowing *how* to defend myself wasn't as revolutionary as giving myself permission to do so. At the time, 9 out of 10 women in America did not fight back during a sexual assault – a quality that assailants looked for when they tested future victims. Self-defense class rewired my belief system to value and assert my boundaries in hopes of merely being a "survivor" in a dangerous world. Creating a world free of sexual assault did not occur to me at that time.

I've been in "survival" mode since I was three -- when dad left. His $600/month child support meant that halfway through the month, money would run out and food insecurity would flood in. I knew that we could buy two large pizzas for $20 back then, so I immediately created my first business. I quickly figured out that if I wore my nurse's outfit from last Halloween, and if I set up a table at the front door, I could charge a nickel to anyone who came in or out, just as I had seen at the doctor's office. I also noticed that small change would get abandoned in the bottom of drawers and old purses. By the end of the week, I had collected $20 and was able to buy two large pizzas.

I'm 55 years-old now, and when anxious, I still eat like there might not be food tomorrow. Although I've been a successful attorney for over 25 years, I still find myself in survival mode more often than I'd like to admit. I only recently realized that our culture's chronic sense of scarcity results from a belief that we are separate from the abundance that the Earth's healthy ecosystems has always offered humanity.

So much abundance in fact, that human population has exponentially grown from 3.7 billion in 1970 when I was born to 8.1 billion today. Even with all the stressors humanity currently faces, human population is expected to increase to over 10 billion over the next 50 years.

Yet, this planet currently produces more oxygen, food and fresh water than we could ever need. The story of scarcity only occurs when I become disconnected from the planet and when I don't see myself as belonging within its abundant ecosystems. If we overfish the ocean and trawl the bottom destroying everything in our path, it will not sustain us in the long run. If, like other creatures on our planet, we only take what we need, don't hoard, and are willing to live symbiotically with the planet, it can easily and abundantly sustain all of us.

I recently planted a forty-foot circular garden in my backyard to test this theory. Never having gardened before, I chose a Syntropic garden approach because I loved the idea that the garden knew best. It was my job to listen. The Amazon rainforest is a great example, where the ecosystem feeds itself through syntropy. Everything works together through relationships and by finding their sweet spot in the forest.

This kind of garden requires me to listen to the plants (instead of my agenda dominating them). It is the gardener's job to discover which plants grow best in the garden in proximity to others, depending on how much light, water and companion plants they desire. The more diversity the better, as each plant has something to offer the others. It's a world where plant material is composted back to the soil to feed the living. It's a world where chemical fertilizers aren't necessary and pest control is naturally handled by diversity and resilience.

Syntropic gardening is the opposite of how we've approached food production in America since the 1950s. Monocrops have depleted the soils rather than fed them. Large scale production has made our food less nutritious, and small scale farmers with diverse crops can no longer compete with large scale production. In addition to genetic modifications, we find ourselves less connected to the land, less nourished by it, and less likely to be able to support ourselves.

Similarly, without fresh water, I would die in about 3 days time. And yet, I cannot tell you where to find a source of fresh water apart from the tap at my sink. What is wrong with this picture? My water is said to come from aquafers on this Big Island of Hawaii, and I pay the county to pump it up for me. If I fail to pay my water bill for more than 30 days, my tap turns off, my shower stop flowing and my toilets stop flushing. Why would any of us give that much power over my life (and death) to a government that forgot to order the parts for five of its wells last year creating an unnecessary water "shortage."

This is an island where millions of gallons of fresh water flows freely to the ocean each day. So many of our beaches bubble with freshwater springs that when you first enter the ocean, the chill sends shivers down your spine. Ancient Hawaiians knew how to gather the fresh water at these springs both at the beach and in the mountains. They knew how to gather fresh water from the rain on the large tropical leaves and from the waterfalls. The word for fresh water, "Wai" when doubled to "Wai Wai" means wealth, prosperity or abundance in the Hawaiiain language. Access to an abundance of free fresh water makes us all feel rich!

At what point did I give my power away to a centralized government well that turns itself off when I fail to pay my water bill in a timely fashion? As someone who was born on this planet, I would think I would learn how to make fire, procure my own water from a natural source and grow my own food by the time I reached my teens. Instead, I find myself feeling legitimately anxious about survival and playing a game called, "I have to go to work so I'm not homeless."

Although we were all born on this planet, someone made up the game of land ownership that legitimizes paying certain people for the privilege of being here. Indigenous cultures did not make up such a game – they remember (like every other species on planet Earth) that they simply belong here.

No wonder homelessness appears to be getting worse in America (increasing 18% in 2024 alone). More and more land is being hoarded and consolidated by those of us who bought into this game (literally). Enough of us have played Monopoly to feel legitimized in pretending that we own the land where we live. In fact, before we made up a different story, land has always been "free" and plentiful to the tribes that stewarded it for thousands of years before us. In America, we currently live on less than half of the land. There is plenty for all, especially when we remember how to live off grid.

Technology makes living off the grid feel luxurious in modern times. We can create our own electricity in a myriad of ways nowadays (mostly solar). We can create our own water out of thin air using atmospheric water generators and by catching the rain. We can take care of our own waste processing using various compact systems.

If everyone lived off grid on this Big Island, we would save $1 billion that we currently need to spend maintaining our centralized sewage plant. These systems are outdated and end up polluting the ocean when there is too much rain or large tides that overwhelm them. We would save an additional $1 billion by not needing to replace our cesspools with septic tanks, most of which don't seem to work well anyway.

The village of Puako here is a great example. Several dozen multi-million dollar homes enjoy their privacy on one of the most beautiful reefs in Hawaii. However, the high bacteria count in the water has long been a nuisance to swimmers and wildlife.

When they tested the septic tanks over a decade ago using dyes, they discovered that raw sewage was seeping into the ocean from just about every house within a few days of the toilet flush. The government gave them over a million dollars to design a wastewater plant for the community. Over a decade later, they have not instituted such a central plan because it is estimated to cost over $14 million more. It appears that the problem for this village cannot be solved by an expensive centralized plan.

In contrast, each toilet could be upgraded to process its own sewage with each flush, solving the problem immediately and inexpensively. If you're wondering why they haven't done so, I believe our system of domination is not just entrenched in government, but also in our own minds. Most Americans have come to believe that the government should provide centralized sewage systems rather than each of us being responsible for our own crap. Even those who own beach homes in Hawaii think that the government should solve their local water quality problem.

We've become accustomed to telling the government that it owes us. The price we pay is chronic anxiety for our very survival. When we give our personal power away to others, and when that power is important for our survival as a human being, we create a potential for one group of people to dominate another. The best use of government in my opinion is to empower its people and protect their personal access to the natural resources rather than allowing monopolies to take advantage of life-supporting resources.

I'll never forget, for example, how California was scammed out of billions of dollars by energy traders while I lived there for 20 years.

The Lesson of the California Blackouts — and the Playbook That Won't Die

In 2000–2001, California faced an energy crisis unlike anything it had seen before. It wasn't caused by a natural disaster. It wasn't a sudden failure of technology. It was *manufactured*.

Energy traders — most infamously at Enron — discovered that if they made electricity appear scarce, the market would reward them with sky-high prices. Power plants went "down for maintenance" during peak demand. Transmission routes were deliberately clogged on paper. With supply choked, wholesale electricity prices soared — sometimes to 20 times the normal rate.

California, desperate to keep the lights on, became the buyer of last resort. In just months, the state went from a $8 billion budget surplus to committing $42 billion in long-term energy contracts, draining the General Fund. The deficits were so deep the state eventually cut $8.1 billion from education spending to plug the holes.

PG&E went bankrupt. Enron's stock collapsed. Traders and executives walked away with millions. A few — like Enron's Timothy Belden — faced charges, but the billions skimmed from California's economy were never fully recovered.

The real blackout wasn't just in our homes — it was in our foresight.

The Playbook

What happened in California was not unique. It was a chapter in a much longer book — a playbook that has been run before, and is still running now. The steps are always the same:

1. **Get control of an essential resource** — energy, homes, medicine, water, even information.
2. **Limit access** — sometimes through real shortages, sometimes just by making it look scarce.
3. **Drive up prices** — because people will pay almost anything to keep the lights on, a roof overhead, or their loved ones alive.
4. **Cash out** — before the public or regulators catch on.
5. **Pay a fine, not the bill** — and walk away with the lion's share of the profits.

Housing

In the early 2000s, banks sold risky mortgages as if they were safe. When the housing bubble burst in 2008, millions lost their homes, but banks got taxpayer bailouts. Today, giant investment firms buy entire neighborhoods of houses, taking them off the market to rent at high rates — holding the housing supply hostage in plain sight.

Medicine

A vial of insulin costs a few dollars to make. In the U.S., it can sell for hundreds. With only a few companies controlling production, prices stay high while patients ration doses, sometimes with deadly results. The product isn't rare — but the *permission* to sell it is.

Electricity — Again

In 2021, Texas froze under an ice storm. Power plants went down, demand spiked, and wholesale electricity prices were allowed to soar to $9,000/MWh. Some providers went bankrupt, others walked away with windfall profits, and many residents faced bills in the thousands for just a few days of heat and light.

Health Care Facilities

Private equity firms buy struggling hospitals, cut staff, and extract profits — sometimes pulling out cash just before closing the doors for good. Communities lose their emergency rooms, but the investors keep the gains.

The Common Thread

Every time, the playbook works because control is centralized **and** the public has no fallback. Whether the gate is guarded by a corporation or a government, whoever holds the keys can name the price — and the rest of us can't simply walk away.

The lesson is the same as it was when California's lights flickered in 2001:
We must build resilient, decentralized systems — many wells, many switches, many paths to what we need. Because as long as we leave our essentials in the hands of a few, we are one "maintenance shutdown" away from being held in the dark again.

From the Illusion of Scarcity to Cooperative Abundance

What happened with Enron was not just a corporate scandal — it was a mirror. It showed us the sickness that grows when we are raised in the myth of separation. We were told life is a competition, that others are rivals, that the measure of success is how much more you have than the next person.

This is domination culture — a culture that trains us to hoard, to climb, to secure our own survival at the expense of others. It is the story that says, "I win when you lose," and in that story, there can never be enough.

But this is not the only story. The deeper truth — the one our bones remember — is that we are part of a living web. In a healthy forest, trees share nutrients through their roots. In a healthy culture, people share wisdom, care, and resources through their relationships.

The antidote to the sickness of domination is cooperation grounded in belonging. It begins with remembering that my well-being and yours are not in competition — they are intertwined. It grows when we design systems where success is measured not by extraction, but by how many are thriving. It becomes unshakable when every person is recognized as an irreplaceable part of the whole.

We do not have to accept a world where a few walk away with fortunes while the many are left in the dark. We can build a culture where no one is left behind, because we understand that to harm one is to harm all — and to lift one is to lift all.

CHAPTER 2

CYCLES OF ABUSE —

THE ONLY CHOICES WE'RE TAUGHT

In the Domination Game, people are trained into one of two roles: dominator or dominated. This is actually just a widespread cycle of abuse where one person (or group) is the abuser, and the other person (or group) is the abused. When someone is bullied, their natural instinct is to resist.

But if the only way we're taught to avoid being bullied is to become the bully, then domination replicates itself like a virus, generation after generation. When we experience this as a group, the "victim story" becomes a story of "oppression" and our anger grows. This anger is healthy because it lets us know we no longer want to play this game. However, if we assume we must become the oppressor to escape the cycle, then our options become very limited indeed.

Unfortunately that is exactly how the trauma cycle repeats itself, not just personally, but collectively. Empires are built on this logic. Institutions replicate it. And we internalize it so much, that at 55 years old, I am writing this book to unveil my own complicity.

The cycle becomes its own form of amnesia. We forget there could be another way. We forget we are more than our wounds.

A great example of this recently occurred when the movie "Barbie" ended with triumphant women causing a war amongst men and taking over the government. Their governmental coup ended with women dominating men and overthrowing a legal system. It wasn't enough that the women in the Barbie movie freed themselves from servitude by unbrainwashing each other, they also had to "win" in a way that our dominant culture (pun intended) could understand. Unfortunately, this result just promised more domination, power struggle, and endless revolutions. That's not the future that makes me want to get out of bed in the morning!

Yes, the first part of this book will expose the rules of the "game," the cost of our participation, and hopefully reveal some blind spots. Don't worry, the second part of this book will bring us out of the murk of the last 8,000 years of Western history, and invite us to join a non-violent revolution that will radically remember our sanity providing relief from much of our suffering.

CHAPTER 3
WHOEVER FRAMES THE ARGUMENT WINS

One of the most powerful tools of domination is framing. Whoever defines the terms of the conversation sets the limits of what is possible. The rules we use to frame society are often called laws. Those who create laws in America are called Congress, and those who enforce that law are lawyers and law enforcement.

Whoever writes the "laws" creates the framework, and that framework is set up to benefit the interests of those who write the laws. Sometimes laws extend to benefit the masses such as civil rights legislation in 1964. It resulted in temporarily stopping the masses from revolting. But having been a civil rights attorney, I can tell you that the civil rights laws are written to be almost impossible to win.

That may sound cynical to most Americans (like me) who hold idealism as a core American value. But having studied law, written and lobbied a law to passage in Congress and enforced our laws as an attorney, I have become disillusioned about our "Justice System." Even when we "won" our cases, and large sums of money were exchanged in the client's favor, our clients never really "won." Clients lives were never better-off in my estimation, and I doubt any of them would ever choose to repeat the process. The law can move money around, but it is terrible at providing real justice.

Let me give you a couple of examples:

1) The courts are structured to "revictimize" the person who was harmed because if everyone is assumed innocent until proven guilty, then our system also assumes that the "victim" is a liar until it is proven that she is not. This is why almost all sexual assailants are never punished. The system is so notoriously stacked against the "victim," that less than 23% of women even bother to report sexual assault.

2) "We the people" to whom the "founding fathers" referred only included about 10% of the United States population at the time. To vote, you had to be (1) white (2) land-owning and (3) male. Around 90% of those living in America were not allowed to participate in the voting process. That's not a democracy.

That's called a plutocracy where a few elites run the show. The charade continues as the electoral college and gerrymandering change the rules behind the scenes.

In the Barbie movie, power was framed by the "constitution" or legal system having power over others to control their behavior. That kind of power is exactly why I became a lawyer in the first place – to obtain it. I was mistaken. Real power and long-term change is never dictated from the top town. It grows like grass from the bottom up.

The country of Turkey is a great example. I had the privilege of living in Istanbul for a year at the age of 19. Their revered leader, Ataturk, legislated many things around 1922. The new laws included the equality of women. That law has yet to be added to America's constitution. My personal experience of being sexually harassed, grabbed and groped in my private areas by total strangers on a daily basis while making my way through the city demonstrated just how little influence the law had on actual practice. Women (like me) submitted in hopes of surviving the brutal consequences of speaking out about this issue. I had heard how brutal the police could be to all parties if sexual assault was reported. Those assaulted could expect to be imprisoned, beaten, sometimes killed by family members to protect the family's honor, or forced to marry the assailant.

I remember my rage fomenting so deeply in Istanbul that after about 9 months of daily assaults on my body, I was ready to kill the next man who touched me. I did everything in my power to avoid men, never to meet their eyes, and I wished I could have worn a full covering to disappear myself into the crowd. After months of abuse and without support to find safer methods of existing, I found myself wanting to harm the misbehaving men. Although I never did respond with violence, I wanted to become the abuser.

If the only options are: dominate or be dominated, then even liberation gets framed as rising to the top of the very same pyramid. But true freedom comes not from flipping roles—it comes from opting out of the game.

We begin by changing the frame. By asking: What if there are more than two choices? What if cooperation, reciprocity, and regeneration aren't just naïve ideals—but our natural way of being before we were conditioned otherwise?

Language of Power:
The Psychology Behind "Having the Upper Hand"

The phrase *"to have the upper hand"* sounds harmless enough. We use it casually—in business meetings, sports, politics, even parenting—to mean that someone has gained an advantage. But this simple idiom reveals a deep cultural imprint: the assumption that one must be *above* to be secure, *in control* to be safe.

Its origins go back to the Middle Ages, when the "upper hand" described literal physical dominance—one hand placed over another in wrestling, swordplay, or even in a game of pulling sticks. The person with the higher hand had the leverage. Power came from position. Control came from pressure. And language, being the vessel of culture, carried this gesture forward into every sphere of life.

Over centuries, it became normal to frame success through the same posture—*over.* We have the upper hand in negotiations, upper management, upper class, upper deck.
Meanwhile, anything *below* implies weakness: underdog, underclass, underling, subordinate.

We may not consciously believe that "up" is good and "down" is bad, yet the association runs through every metaphor we use:

- "Rise to the top."
- "Climb the ladder."
- "Look down on."
- "Step up, not step aside."

Our bodies have learned the hierarchy before our minds could name it.

The Internalized Dominator

Once we begin to see how deeply the domination framework is woven into language, we recognize how subtly it shapes our inner worlds. Many of us were raised to believe that to survive, we must stay "on top" of things—our emotions, our finances, our relationships, our competitors, even our own bodies.

The result is a constant vigilance, an unconscious gripping against the imagined danger of "falling behind." This tension breeds exhaustion, comparison, control, and the fear of vulnerability. We begin to dominate ourselves before anyone else needs to.

That is the true genius—and tragedy—of domination culture: when the system no longer needs to police us, because we've internalized the policing.

Breaking the Spell

The good news is that unlearning domination is not an act of rebellion against others—it's a return to balance within ourselves. The language we use, the metaphors we live by, can become doorways to freedom rather than cages.

Here are a few ways to begin reprogramming the domination mindset:

1. **Notice your metaphors.**
   Each time you hear yourself or others say "climb," "beat," "win," or "get ahead," pause. Ask: *Is there another way to describe success?* Try replacing "getting ahead" with "growing together" or "rising in harmony."

2. **Practice power-with instead of power-over.**
   When you feel the urge to control—whether in conversation, parenting, or work—experiment with curiosity instead. Ask: *What wants to emerge between us, not just from me?*

3. **Reclaim your body from hierarchy.**
   Take slow breaths. Feel the weight of your feet on the ground. Soften the shoulders that try to stay "up." Your body already knows how to be in balance, not battle.

4. **Use collaborative language.**
   Replace competition with cooperation: "Let's explore this," "Let's build together," "How can we both thrive?" Language

doesn't just describe reality—it creates it.

5. **Celebrate circular success.**
   In place of ladders, picture circles, spirals, ecosystems. Every being contributes to the whole. The tree doesn't "win" over the soil—it grows *because* of it.

Reframing the Frame

If domination lives in the metaphors we've inherited, liberation lives in the metaphors we choose next. When we speak of **power-with** instead of **power-over**, we begin to change not only how we relate to others— but how we perceive the very nature of life.

Because the truth is: no one can "have" the upper hand in a living ecosystem. There is no top in a circle.

CHAPTER 4
THE MYTH OF SURVIVAL OF THE FITTEST

We've been taught a distorted view of evolution, focused only on competition. "Survival of the fittest" became a justification for every kind of ruthless behavior. But Darwin also observed the importance of cooperation, of symbiosis. Bees and flowers. Mycelial networks and trees. Herd animals who protect the vulnerable.

Human beings are not lone wolves—we are hive creatures. Culture creators. Our most prosperous civilizations have thrived when cooperation and trust flourished.

But conflict theory infected everything—from history textbooks focused only on wars, to board games like Monopoly that reward bankrupting other players. For generations, we were taught that life is a ruthless contest — that only the strongest survive. This story seeped into our politics, our economies, and even our sense of self. But it was never the whole truth.

When Charles Darwin observed the living world, what astonished him most was *relationship*. He wrote of "mutual aid" among animals, of symbiotic webs that bound species together. Yet when the Industrial Age took hold, the idea of "survival of the fittest" was seized by those who already saw life as a hierarchy. Herbert Spencer, not Darwin, coined the phrase — and used it to justify empire, capitalism, and class rule. The notion that domination was "natural" became a convenient story for those who benefited from it.

In truth, evolution is a dance of *cooperation*. The strongest do not survive; the most connected do. From coral reefs to rainforests, from human families to microbial communities, life organizes itself through reciprocity. Biologist Lynn Margulis showed that the very cells in our bodies arose from ancient symbioses — unions of once-separate organisms learning to live as one.

Even the human brain bears this signature of unity. Mirror neurons light up when we witness another's joy or pain. Empathy isn't a moral luxury; it's a survival mechanism. We are evolution made conscious — the universe remembering itself through relationship.

Yet we built societies on a distortion — a belief that to dominate is to thrive. This story made us lonely. It fractured our connection to nature and to each other, replacing belonging with competition. But every generation brings new evidence that the story was false. Cooperation, generosity, and compassion are not anomalies; they are the code of life itself.

To free ourselves from the domination game, we must rewrite the story of human nature. Not as conquerors of the Earth, but as participants in her symphony. The next evolution of humanity will not come through control, but through cooperation. It begins when we remember that our truest instinct is not to fight for survival — it is to love for life.

Here's an ancient story that demonstrates this alternative narrative.

The Four Harmonious Friends

In a forest long ago, four animals—a partridge, a rabbit, a monkey, and an elephant—wondered who among them should lead. Each had a reason to claim the top branch of the hierarchy: the elephant for its strength, the monkey for its cleverness, the rabbit for its speed, and the partridge for its song.

But rather than fight, they decided to ask a deeper question: *How can each of us serve so that all may flourish?*

They discovered that the partridge had first seen the seed of the great tree that shaded them all. The rabbit had watered it, the monkey had tended its young shoots, and the elephant had protected it as it grew. The tree existed because of their shared effort.

So they climbed it together—the partridge on the rabbit, the rabbit on the monkey, the monkey on the elephant. From that height, all could see farther. All could eat of the fruit. All could rest in the shade. None were less; none were more.

In this way, they became known as *The Four Harmonious Friends*, symbols of interdependence and collective wisdom throughout Buddhist art and story.

Their lesson is simple: no one leads when everyone contributes. Power does not belong to the biggest or loudest; it belongs to the ecosystem of cooperation.

Reflection: From Hierarchy to Harmony

The Four Harmonious Friends embody the very principle of power-with. Each being's strength becomes nourishment for the others. Diversity becomes resilience. Relationship becomes wealth.

This is the natural law that domination forgot.
No tree grows alone. No ocean wave rises without the tide.

If the old story of domination was built on ladders, the new story is built on circles.

As we move toward a future of shared sovereignty—where ownership is redefined as stewardship, where all belong and we remember that liberation isn't about rising above others. It's about rising *with* others.

CHAPTER 5

WHY HUMANS COOPERATE — SURVIVAL BY TRUST, NOT TYRANNY

"We are soft animals who survived a hard world because we learned to care for one another." — Anonymous

The Great Human Paradox

Humans are born the most helpless of all mammals.
We enter the world hairless, slow, and dependent—unable to walk, feed, or defend ourselves. A newborn foal can stand within hours; a human child takes nearly a year. We lack claws, fangs, armor, or camouflage. By nature's standards, we are fragile.

And yet—against all odds—we became the most adaptive species on Earth.

How?
Not by claw, but by connection.
Not by domination, but by cooperation.
Not by survival of the fittest, but by survival of the kindest.

From the very beginning, our survival depended on our ability to trust, share, and care. Our biology makes this clear: our brains are wired for empathy, our hormones reward collaboration, our language evolved to coordinate and imagine together. If competition sharpened our minds, cooperation gave us meaning.

The Evolutionary Advantage of Empathy

In the ancestral wild, isolation meant death. To thrive, we needed others—to hunt, to raise children, to defend the campfire. Early humans who cooperated were more likely to survive, and their offspring carried forward the same social instincts.

We don't just raise our own children—we raise each other's.

24

That impulse for collective caregiving may have been the foundation of civilization itself. Mutual aid wasn't idealism; it was survival strategy.

Groups that shared food, knowledge, and protection fared better than groups ruled by domination and fear. The most successful societies didn't rely on alpha males—they relied on shared leadership, reciprocal trust, and collective intelligence.

Nature's Law of Interdependence

Everything alive participates in a network of mutual benefit.
The forest thrives because trees share nutrients through underground fungal networks. Coral reefs flourish through symbiosis. Wolves maintain ecological balance not through conquest but coordination.

Human beings are no different. We are not separate from nature's cooperative web—we are one of its most intricate expressions. Domination is an aberration—a brief detour from nature's long experiment with interdependence.

When we live by extraction, we destroy the very relationships that sustain us. When we live by reciprocity, life multiplies around us.

The Rise of the "Mutual Brain"

Neuroscience now confirms what indigenous wisdom and myth have long taught: our brains are not designed for solitary survival—they are designed for interconnection.

Mirror neurons allow us to feel one another's emotions. Oxytocin rewards bonding and trust. Even our sense of self—our "I"—is shaped by "we." In other words, we became human together.

Our ancestors sang in groups to synchronize movement. We painted cave walls to tell shared stories. We buried our dead, revealing our capacity to grieve and remember collectively. Culture itself was born from cooperation.

Domination, by contrast, isolates. It fractures the collective mind and turns shared strength into fear-based control. Over time, this weakens societies from within.

Survival by Trust

When tyrannies fall, it is not the strongest who rebuild—it is the most cooperative. Every great renewal in human history—be it the Renaissance, civil rights, or the rise of open-source technology—has emerged from people choosing to trust, share, **and** collaborate beyond imposed boundaries.

Trust is not naivety. It is the foundation of civilization.

We trust the baker to bake our bread. We trust the driver to stay in their lane. We trust the stranger who designed the bridge to make it safe. Every act of cooperation is a quiet act of faith in the human story. And every betrayal of that trust—be it corruption, greed, or domination—fractures the collective field of possibility.

From Power-Over to Power-With

Domination arose when humans forgot that power-with is stronger than power-over. The conqueror's power isolates him; the collaborator's power multiplies. Just as cells in a body cooperate to sustain life, so do communities thrive when each part contributes to the whole.

We are only as strong as the trust between us. When we exploit others, we weaken ourselves. When we lift others, we all rise.

That is the great irony of evolution: We became the most successful species on the planet not by killing the competition, but by expanding the circle of cooperation until it included *everyone*—and, someday, perhaps *everything*.

The New Story of Survival

The next chapter of humanity depends on remembering what made us human in the first place: our capacity to care, to share, and to belong.

The old story of survival of the fittest has run its course. The new story is survival of the most connected.

To thrive in the age ahead, we must shift from the myth of dominance to the reality of reciprocity—from extraction to regeneration, from isolation to interbeing. When we work *with* nature instead of *against* it, when we trust the wisdom in one another, we rejoin the living web from which we came.

And from there, anything becomes possible.

As an anthropology major, I've always been interested in studying cultures that have something profound to teach us, especially when doubters try to discourage my optimism. To know that other cultures have already accomplished a symbiotic relationship with each other and the Earth is to know that is possible. The next chapter provides some examples.

CHAPTER 6
THE FORGOTTEN SOCIETIES OF TRUST AND WHY THEY MUST BE REMEMBERED

"It is no measure of health to be well adjusted to a profoundly sick society."
—Jiddu Krishnamurti

When we imagine human history, we are taught to remember its conquerors—Alexander the Great, Napoleon, the kings, the generals, the patriarchs. But behind every empire stood something older and quieter: the great cooperative cultures that made civilization possible long before the age of domination.

Beneath the shadow of conquest, there has always been another story—of people who chose *trust* over tyranny, *reciprocity* over rule, and *shared wisdom* over one-man power. Let's remember them.

The Egalitarian Bands — Humanity's First Social Order

For most of our species' existence—over 90% of it—humans lived in small, mobile, egalitarian bands. The Hadza of Tanzania still reflect this ancient pattern: they make decisions by open discussion, not decree. No one hoards food; hunters share the day's catch, and even successful gatherers distribute fruits evenly across the group. If one person boasts or tries to dominate, gentle teasing restores humility and harmony.

These bands function through social checks and emotional intelligence, not coercion. Their moral compass is calibrated by belonging: if you harm others, you harm the web that sustains you. Anthropologist James Suzman calls this the "original economy of enough."

This way of life—consensus-based, flexible, and fluid—isn't primitive. It's *adaptive*. It kept humanity alive through ice ages, migrations, and droughts because trust was the true currency of survival.

The Stateless Societies — The Power of Consensus

Across Africa, many cultures evolved without centralized rule or kingship. The Igbo of Nigeria, for instance, operated for centuries as an acephalous society—meaning "headless." Villages were governed by councils of elders, but leadership rotated and decisions emerged through patient deliberation. The goal was not victory, but harmony.

Similarly, the Nuer of South Sudan practiced decentralized governance, resolving disputes through respected mediators rather than permanent rulers. Power was relational, not positional.

These societies remind us that *organization without domination* is possible. They held structure without coercion, unity without uniformity—a living example of what modern theorists might call "distributed governance."

The Piaroa of the Amazon — Harmony as Law

In the Venezuelan rainforest, the Piaroa people live by a philosophy that might as well be humanity's lost instruction manual. They actively resist aggression, viewing anger and greed as forms of spiritual pollution. Among them, status-seeking is treated as a mental illness that threatens the balance of the group. Every adult has a say in decisions. Wisdom is shared horizontally, and spiritual practices focus on keeping desire in balance with gratitude. No one dominates, because doing so would rupture their sacred web of reciprocity—with one another *and* with the forest that feeds them.

The Piaroa prove that peace is not naïve—it's *discipline*.

The Sakuddei of Indonesia — Equality as Everyday Life

The Sakuddei of the Mentawai Islands have no chiefs, no warriors, and no prisons. They live in extended family groups where decisions are made communally, and gender equality is woven into daily life. When conflict arises, they resolve it through song and storytelling—a tradition that transforms emotion into understanding.

There is no concept of owning land or people; the forest belongs to itself, and they belong to it. In their culture, leadership is not about control—it's about coherence.

The Iroquois Confederacy — A Government of Balance and Wisdom

Long before the United States existed, an alliance of Indigenous nations in the northeastern woodlands of North America created one of the most sophisticated democracies in human history. The Iroquois, or *Haudenosaunee* — "the People of the Longhouse" — transformed a landscape of violence into a living covenant of peace.

Five warring tribes — the Mohawk, Oneida, Onondaga, Cayuga, and Seneca — had been trapped in cycles of revenge until a visionary known as the Peacemaker traveled among them carrying a single message: *unity is strength*. Through his guidance and the wisdom of the clan mother Jikonsahseh and the healing story of Hiawatha, the tribes chose to unite rather than destroy each other. They buried their weapons beneath the roots of a great white pine — the Tree of Peace — and formed the Haudenosaunee Confederacy, governed by the Great Law of Peace.

Under this law, decisions were made through consensus, not conquest. Each nation kept its own sovereignty, yet joined in a larger federation for mutual protection and prosperity. The Great Law established a three-part structure of governance — a council of representatives, a balance of powers, and codified rights of speech and conscience. Centuries later, the framers of the United States Constitution would study this model and adapt many of its principles — particularly the federal structure that balanced state independence with shared oversight.

But they left behind its heart.

Among the Haudenosaunee, power was not a privilege to be seized but a responsibility to be earned. The chiefs, or sachems, were chosen by the clan mothers — the grandmothers — who served as the moral guardians of the people. Leadership was an appointment to serve, not a path to wealth. There were no salaries, no titles of nobility, no dynasties of inheritance. And if a chief abused his authority or acted without integrity, the same grandmother who raised him to leadership could remove him with a symbolic gesture: the shaking of her wampum belt.

Property, too, was passed matrilineally — through the women who sustained the families and the land. This ensured a natural balance between masculine and feminine energies of governance. Neither ruled the other. They ruled *with* one another.

When the founders of the American republic borrowed the Iroquois model, they took its outer form — the three branches of government — but not its inner harmony. They left out the women and therefore the grandmothers.. They built a structure of power without the wisdom that softens power into stewardship. In doing so, they planted the seeds of domination even within a system meant for liberty.

For centuries, the Great Law of Peace sustained the Iroquois nations through war, famine, and colonization because it was rooted in relationship, not hierarchy. Its foundation was trust, not fear. Its currency was respect, not control. In that design, we glimpse what human governance can become again — not a game of domination, but a living balance of feminine and masculine intelligence, reason and compassion, autonomy and belonging.

If America is to heal its divisions, it must remember what its own founders forgot: that the true measure of democracy is not how loudly it declares freedom, but how deeply it listens to wisdom – including feminine wisdom.

The Cooperative Principle of Survival

Across continents and millennia, these societies share a single insight: Strength is not domination—it is connection. Their people survived not because they conquered, but because they *cooperated*. Because they trusted the unseen threads of reciprocity that hold life together.

Modern science now echoes what these ancient societies embodied. Our ancestors who cooperated were more likely to eat, survive, reproduce, and pass on their cooperative genes.
Trust became biology; empathy became evolution.

Even today, our bodies reward cooperation with dopamine and oxytocin—the same neurochemicals that signal love and joy. Domination floods us with cortisol and adrenaline—chemicals meant for short bursts of survival, not long-term flourishing.

When we live by domination, we live in permanent emergency. When we live by cooperation, we live in the rhythm of creation.

Remembering the Original Template

These examples are not nostalgic relics—they are *reminders of our blueprint.* The human story did not begin with empire. It began around campfires, with songs, sharing, and laughter—long before the first fortress was built.

The myth of the "alpha male" is a late invention, a distortion of the true human pattern. The most successful societies didn't rely on alphas—they relied on shared leadership, reciprocal trust, and collective intelligence.

And perhaps that is why humanity's next evolutionary leap will not come from artificial intelligence or space travel, but from remembering what made us human in the first place: We survived by caring for one another.

Why the Gentle Are Often Forgotten

Skeptics might argue:
"If cooperative societies were truly superior, they would have survived. If the peaceful were so wise, why were they conquered by the violent? Surely domination wins, or we wouldn't be here."

It's an understandable conclusion—but a short-sighted one.

The Short View: Domination as Visible Power

History, as it's usually told, is written by the victors. We celebrate conquerors because their power leaves monuments, not because it leaves wisdom. Empires burn their mark into stone; cooperative cultures grow quietly in living soil. When one is crushed, its spirit disperses and takes root elsewhere, invisible to historians but alive in the DNA of human kindness.

Domination survives by force and fear; cooperation survives by regeneration and renewal. Like grass after fire, it always grows back. Domination looks strong because it's loud, fast, and dramatic. But it depends on a constant supply of energy to suppress rebellion.
It can never rest, because it rules against the natural law of balance.

Cooperation looks fragile because it's soft, quiet, and slow.
Yet it's what makes the soil fertile again after the empire collapses.
Domination builds fortresses; cooperation builds ecosystems.

The Long View: The Silent Victories of the Cooperative Spirit

Every empire that rose through domination has fallen—Egyptian, Roman, British, Soviet. But the cooperative cultures they tried to erase—tribes, villages, monastic orders, farmers' guilds, local communities—still exist in new forms. They keep the pulse of life going while the conquerors' monuments crumble.

In the long arc of evolution, it is *interdependence* that endures.

Just as species that over-consume their environment go extinct, civilizations that over-exploit others inevitably collapse. Survival through domination is a sprint; survival through cooperation is a marathon.

The Gandhi Principle: Non-Violent Power as Evolutionary Strength

When Gandhi faced the British Empire—the largest, richest, most militarized system of domination in human history—he had no armies, no guns, and no throne. Yet, he knew how to free India from British rule. He was armed with a truth so powerful it could not be conquered:

> *"In the midst of darkness, light persists.*
> *In the midst of untruth, truth persists.*
> *In the midst of death, life persists."*

Gandhi's genius was that he refused to play the domination game. He did not fight to overthrow the British through violence; he exposed the moral bankruptcy of domination itself. By choosing non-violent resistance—satyagraha, or "truth-force"—he reframed power as something arising from integrity, not intimidation.

The British Empire could defeat an army but not a conscience. It could control a body but not a soul. By enduring suffering without inflicting it, Gandhi revealed the absurdity of domination and won the only victory that lasts—the awakening of collective moral vision.

The British left India not because they were destroyed, but because they were transformed—because millions of people chose to cooperate in non-cooperation.

That paradox is the key:
Gandhi's "resistance" was not destruction—it was withdrawal of consent from an abusive system, so that a new cooperative order could rise in its place.

The Lesson for Us Today

The domination mindset says:
"To win, you must overpower."

The cooperative mindset says:
"To heal, you must outlast."

One burns fast; the other burns eternal.

Gandhi's victory is not an anomaly—it's a demonstration of nature's law. True power does not dominate. It *resonates*. It harmonizes individuals into movements, movements into nations, and nations into new stories of belonging.

Domination has ruled history's headlines; cooperation has ruled history's survival. One day, perhaps, they will finally be seen as the same story—the old world's last scream and the new world's first song.

CHAPTER 7
COOPERATION IN THE CONTEXT OF CONFLICT

At first glance, war appears to prove that domination works. Armies are built on command hierarchies, discipline, obedience, and control. Victory is measured in who submits first.
But beneath every successful military operation lies an invisible truth: warfare itself depends on cooperation.

Even War Runs on Cooperation

No army can function without trust—between soldiers, between units, between leaders and those they lead. Each battle plan depends on synchronization, timing, communication, and mutual reliability. In other words, cooperation is the lifeblood of domination systems, even if it is rarely acknowledged as such.

When cooperation fails, domination collapses under its own weight. General George Custer's defeat at Little Bighorn (1876) is a textbook case: his success depended on three other regiments coordinating their movements. When those units failed to arrive on time—due to miscommunication, poor planning, or fractured trust—Custer's isolated force was surrounded by the combined Lakota, Northern Cheyenne, and Arapaho warriors. Domination failed not because his men lacked courage, but because they lacked *cohesion.*

It was not aggression that doomed Custer—it was the breakdown of cooperation.

The Cooperative Intelligence of the Lakota and Cheyenne

In contrast, the Native coalition at Little Bighorn demonstrated a form of collective intelligence rooted in cooperation rather than command. Multiple tribes, each autonomous and proud, came together under a shared cause: defending their land and way of life. They didn't operate under a single general. They coordinated through trust, shared purpose, and mutual respect for each group's strengths. That unity—what the

35

U.S. military would call "interoperability"—was precisely what Custer lacked.

Domination isolates; cooperation integrates.

The Native alliance's victory that day wasn't merely tactical—it was philosophical. It proved that cooperation, even among fiercely independent peoples, can outmaneuver domination when aligned with shared purpose.

The Paradox of Power

This pattern repeats across history. Some empires arose through force, but they were only stable when they establish cooperation among the governed. Revolutions succeed not because they dominate, but because they inspire *collective will*. In that sense, domination is not the opposite of cooperation—it is a distortion of it. It takes the connective power of cooperation and uses it for control rather than creation. The best victory is one achieved without battle—by aligning hearts and minds so thoroughly that resistance dissolves. That is the art of cooperative power.

The Gandhi Parallel

Just as Custer's failure reveals the collapse of cooperation under domination, Gandhi's triumph reveals its rebirth. Both faced conflict; both had followers; both required strategy. But where Custer commanded, Gandhi invited. Where Custer demanded obedience, Gandhi evoked conscience.

Gandhi proved that cooperative strength can end empires without violence. His "army" had no weapons, yet it moved as one body—a living organism of shared purpose. Each person acted independently, yet in harmony with the whole.

This is collective sovereignty in action—power-with, not power-over.

The Lesson: Cooperation is Not Weakness, It's Mastery

The misconception that cooperation equals weakness comes from confusing *gentleness* with *passivity*. In truth, cooperation is what allows any complex system—natural or human—to endure stress, adapt, and regenerate. It's the principle of resilience through relationship.

When domination breaks down, cooperation is what rebuilds. It is the connective tissue of life itself—the reason humanity survived storms, famines, and wars far longer than any empire did. Even the military, at its best, depends not on fear but on unit cohesion—a word that literally means "to bind together."

So the question isn't whether cooperation can withstand conflict. The real question is whether domination can survive *without* cooperation.

It never has.

Human Nature is Mostly Good

We've been conditioned to believe that, left to our own devices, humans would devolve into chaos—like in *Lord of the Flies*. But anthropological evidence suggests the opposite. In crises, humans often cooperate. In villages, people care for each other. Most of us just want to belong, to be safe, to love and be loved.

Domination is not our nature—it is our trauma.

And when trauma is healed, our true nature resurfaces: empathy, creativity, generosity.

> *"You may shoot me with your words, you may cut me with your eyes, you may kill me with your hatefulness, but still, like air, I'll rise!"*
> — Maya Angelou

CHAPTER 8

THE FEAR FACTORY — HOW THE DOMINATION GAME CONTROLS THE MIND

"Men are not ruled by truth,
but by the stories they believe about danger."
— Anonymous

The Old Currency Of Control

For most of human history, fear was not our organizing principle —
trust was. We lived in kinship societies, sustained by reciprocity and
mutual care, where survival depended on cooperation, not control. For
hundreds of thousands of years, humans thrived as gatherers,
gardeners, and stewards of the land, guided by story, ceremony, and
belonging.

Only in the last small fraction of our history — the brief eight-
thousand-year blip of patriarchy — did the Domination Game emerge.
Fear became the new currency of power. As hierarchical systems
spread, rulers learned that the surest way to control a people was to
shape their imagination. By teaching what to fear — and whom to obey
— they redefined what it meant to survive. The myths of domination
began to replace the memory of cooperation, turning obedience into a
virtue and submission into safety.

During the Middle Ages, this tactic was refined and codified. In 1513,
Niccolò Machiavelli's *The Prince* gave rulers a manual for maintaining
control through fear, deception, and manipulation — not moral
authority. He wrote that it was "safer to be feared than loved,"
capturing the essence of the Domination Game in a single phrase.
Centuries later, his logic still echoes in the tyrant's playbook — in
politics, media, corporate hierarchies, and even social systems that prize
compliance over conscience. The strategy remains the same: keep the
people afraid, and they will police themselves.

Every domination system, ancient or modern, feeds on this reflex. Fear
tightens the body, narrows the mind, and collapses complexity into two

choices: fight or flee. In that contracted state, we stop questioning who benefits from our terror.

Modern fear wears a new disguise. It arrives not as the roar of lions at the cave mouth, but as headlines, tweets, and breaking news banners that flash red to mimic blood. It whispers through our devices, telling us that chaos is everywhere and that we must cling to those who promise control.

When fear becomes the organizing principle of a culture, the people no longer need to be chained. They will guard their own cages, convinced the bars keep them safe.

The Manufacture of Panic

In the digital age, fear is no longer a byproduct of domination—it's a business model.

The 24-hour news cycle depends on outrage for profit. Social media platforms track our anxieties like predators track scent. The more we click, the more fear we're fed. The algorithm learns to press our emotional buttons faster than any dictator ever could.

Psychologists call this Mean World Syndrome: the more violence we see on screens, the more dangerous we believe the world to be. Even if crime rates drop, our nervous systems remain convinced we're under siege. Fear becomes not an emotion, but an atmosphere.

This is how millions come to believe that their own neighbors are enemies, that their cities are "war zones," or that only an iron-fisted ruler can protect them. When a population is terrified, authoritarianism can masquerade as safety.

It is not that we are naïve. We are responding rationally to an irrational information environment. Our nervous systems are being hacked. Fear is being coded into the culture as a normal operating system.

Once a population has internalized fear as its default state, domination doesn't need to enforce obedience. People will beg for it.

When Love Turns to Loyalty

To understand why so many good-hearted people fall under the spell of fear-based authority, we must look deeper than politics. The human nervous system is built for belonging. When the world feels unsafe, our primal instinct is to seek protection—usually from a strong figure who promises certainty.

This is why authoritarian movements often present themselves as paternal or patriotic. "Trust me," says the strongman, "I will protect you. I am the only one who can fix this." The promise of safety feels like love, but it is love with conditions—love that demands obedience in return.

For someone who feels isolated, this promise is magnetic. It offers community, purpose, and clarity in a world that feels confusing. The "in-group" becomes family. Loyalty replaces critical thinking. To question the leader feels like betrayal.

But loyalty rooted in fear is not belonging—it is bondage. It trades the intimacy of shared humanity for the security of shared enemies.

When we emerge from this trance, we will want to bring our loved ones with us. To do so we must remember: underneath the ideology is longing. A longing to feel safe, to be part of something meaningful, to know who to trust in a world that feels unstable. The way out is not argument, but re-connection.

The Feedback Loop of Fear

The domination system depends on what I call the feedback loop of fear:

1. **Fear is amplified.** Emotional stories of danger, crime, or invasion flood the media stream.

2. **Trust is eroded.** Neighbors, teachers, journalists, and even family members become potential threats.

3. **Authority is invited.** In the name of safety, we welcome surveillance, censorship, or militarization.

4. **Freedom contracts.** With each emergency, rights are "temporarily" suspended, often never to return.

5. **Fear renews itself.** The same authorities who claim to protect us keep the fear alive to justify their power.

This cycle can continue indefinitely, even in democracies, because fear feels moral. When we are afraid, we believe we are defending the good. The brain confuses vigilance with virtue.

The genius of the domination game is that it convinces us we are fighting evil, when we are really just fighting one another. The system doesn't care who wins, as long as fear keeps the game alive.

Breaking the Spell

Breaking free from the fear factory is not about ignoring real dangers. It's about reclaiming the clarity to see which threats are real and which are manufactured. It's about recognizing when fear is being used as a lever of control rather than as a call to awareness.

Here are a few ways we can begin:

1. Question the Source, Not the Symptom.

When a story triggers outrage or panic, pause. Ask: Who benefits from my fear? Fear is never neutral—it always serves someone's agenda.

2. **Ground in the Body.**

When fear takes hold, the body contracts. Soften the shoulders. Feel your breath. Step outside. Remember that the sky is not falling—it is expanding.

3. **Seek Lived Reality, Not Virtual Drama.**

Look around your neighborhood. Talk to real people. Most are kind, generous, and doing their best. The world of screens is not the world of streets.

4. **Replace Reaction with Curiosity.**

Curiosity dissolves fear like sunlight dissolves fog. Ask questions. Listen. When people feel heard, their need to defend diminishes. That's how bridges are built.

5. **Create Safe Circles.**

The antidote to the culture of fear is community. Gather small groups to share stories, meals, and perspectives. When we feel safe together, fear loses its grip.

How to Help Those We Love

When someone we care about has been captured by fear-based narratives, our instinct is often to confront or correct them. But confrontation only reinforces the siege mentality. Instead, we must approach them the way sunlight approaches ice—warmly, patiently, without force.

1) **Begin with empathy.** Say, "I know you're scared. I feel that way sometimes too." This validates the emotion without endorsing the story.

2) **Ask questions rather than give answers.** "What sources have you found most trustworthy?" "Do you think all of them could be mistaken sometimes?" Questions open space where certainty had closed it.

3) **Find shared values.** Everyone wants safety, belonging, and dignity. The moment you name a value you both cherish, the wall between you softens.

4) **Share calm energy, not facts.** Fear is contagious, but so is serenity. Speak from peace. The body recognizes truth through resonance more than rhetoric.

5) **Model courage.** Show, don't tell, what it looks like to live unafraid. People may forget what you said, but they will remember how you made them feel.

Remember: you cannot argue someone out of fear. But you can love them out of isolation. And isolation is what fear feeds on most.

The New Story of Safety

The greatest illusion of the domination game is that safety can be enforced. True safety is not the absence of threat—it is the presence of trust.

We are safest not when we are guarded, but when we are connected. Not when we build walls, but when we build relationships strong enough to weather misunderstanding.

Safety born of fear breeds control.
Safety born of love breeds cooperation.

Fear says: Obey.
Love says: Belong.

Every major spiritual tradition has taught this in some form. Christ said, "Perfect love casts out fear." The Buddha taught that liberation arises when we see clearly, without craving or aversion. Indigenous elders remind us that fear dissolves when we remember our place within the web of life.

The domination system wants us to forget that. It wants us anxious, divided, and distracted. Because a fearful population is predictable. But a connected population is ungovernable by manipulation. The moment we realize that no one can sell us safety, the market for fear collapses.

From Domination to Liberation

Every time we choose curiosity over outrage, compassion over contempt, connection over control, we unplug another wire from the fear machine. The courage to stay open is the quiet revolution of our time. It doesn't march or shout. It breathes. It listens. It remembers that the world is not ending—it is asking to be reborn.

The opposite of fear is not bravery. It is intimacy. When we know ourselves and one another deeply enough, no propaganda can make us enemies again. This is the turning point of human evolution: from obedience to awareness, from protectionism to participation, from domination to belonging.

I'm not suggesting that crime, rape and theft doesn't happen, or that we should not take precautions. I'm saying we should be aware of how the media spins those stories so we can have a more accurate view of humanity's magnificence.

"You must not lose faith in humanity. Humanity is an ocean; if a few drops of the ocean are dirty, the ocean does not become dirty." -- Mahatma Gandhi

CHAPTER 9

OPTING OUT OF THE MACHINE — FROM EMPLOYMENT TO SOVEREIGNTY

"The rich cannot accumulate wealth without the co-operation of the poor in society."
— Mahatma Gandhi, 1927

The Invisible Empire of Employment

Modern society prides itself on freedom. We can vote, travel, and choose our careers. Yet the most powerful form of control in our time doesn't come from kings or tyrants—it comes from economic dependency.

The *employment system* has quietly replaced monarchy as the dominant form of human subjugation. It promises stability while breeding insecurity, rewards obedience more than creativity, and cloaks servitude in the language of opportunity.

To earn a living, most of us sell our life energy to systems that do not love us. We spend our best hours building someone else's dream, producing more wealth for those who already have enough, while being told we should be grateful for the privilege.

Employment is not inherently evil—but the way it's structured today reflects the old logic of domination: a few control the many, deciding who is "essential," who is expendable, and what our time is worth.

The Birth of Labor as Resistance

When the imbalance of power became unbearable during the Industrial Revolution, workers began to organize. Labor unions were born from a cry for dignity—the recognition that human beings are not machines and that their labor carries moral weight.

By striking, marching, and bargaining collectively, they sought to humanize the factory floor. This was an early expression of *collective sovereignty*: the belief that ordinary people, united in purpose, could rebalance the scales.

Unions taught the world that when workers cooperate, they become powerful. Yet they remained trapped in a paradox—they were still playing on the dominator's board, fighting for fairness inside a system designed to commodify them. Their victories improved conditions, but the structure remained intact: one side owned the means of production; the other side *rented its survival.*

The Gandhi Path — Non-Cooperation with Dependence

Gandhi saw the same pattern under British rule. India's subjugation wasn't sustained by guns—it was sustained by compliance. Every time Indians bought British cloth or salt, they strengthened the system that exploited them.

His solution was revolutionary in its simplicity: withdraw cooperation. He called it *Swadeshi*—the practice of self-sufficiency, of producing locally what one needs, and of refusing to depend on an exploitative empire.

When Gandhi walked to the sea to make salt with his own hands, he was not just defying a law—he was dissolving the illusion of dependence. He showed that true freedom is not won by overthrowing rulers but by reclaiming the ability to meet one's own needs.

> *"When the people withdraw their cooperation, the government cannot exist."*
> — Gandhi, 1930

We face the same choice today—mostly against an empire of corporations who rely on consumers (us).

The Quiet Revolution of Cottage Industry

The way out of the employer–employee cycle is not rebellion—it's *reinvention.* When we build small, resilient economies based on cottage industry, cooperative enterprise, and local reciprocity, we step off the treadmill of dependence. We rediscover the natural dignity of work— where the one who creates also benefits directly from creation.

A *cottage industry* is more than a business model; it's a philosophy. It says:

- "I will not trade my creativity for survival."
- "I will make something beautiful and useful."
- "I will share my surplus, not my sovereignty."

Imagine communities where:

- Homes are powered by solar energy and water catchment systems.
- Gardens and local food co-ops replace supermarket dependency.
- Artisans and digital creators trade directly with customers, without intermediaries (think artisan markets and Etsy).
- Micro-factories and 3D printing workshops bring manufacturing back to neighborhoods.
- Local currencies and time banks circulate value within the community (think credit unions and micro loans).
- Grocery stores are co-ops and farmer's markets.

These are not utopian dreams—they are happening now.
The tools of decentralization, from renewable tech to blockchain (cryptocurrency), make Gandhi's *Swadeshi* possible again on a global scale.

From Labor to Love

The industrial era trained us to believe that work must be toil. But *labor* and *livelihood* are not the same. Labor is what we do to survive; livelihood is what we do to *serve life*.

When we return to cottage-scale creation, our work becomes sacred again. We no longer measure success in money, but in meaning. Profit becomes purpose fulfilled—not power gained.

And when each of us produces something of real value—whether food, beauty, knowledge, or care—we no longer need to "earn" our place in the world. We already belong.

A Sovereign Future

To opt out of the domination economy does not mean retreating from society—it means *rebuilding it from the roots up*.

We can choose:

- **Self-reliance over subservience.**
- **Collaboration over competition.**
- **Regeneration over extraction.**

We can form small, sovereign communities that thrive through shared resources and reciprocal abundance. We can teach our children that the purpose of work is not to climb a ladder, but to *weave a web*. In the end, the employer–employee dynamic is not just an economic relationship— it's a mirror of humanity's collective belief in dependency. When that belief dissolves, so does the illusion of power. The machine runs only as long as we keep feeding it.

When we walk away—together—the world changes.

That can sound like a pipe dream when one relies on the 9 to 5 job to put food on the table. So let's explore . . .

What Makes True Sovereignty Possible?

Real freedom—true sovereignty—requires more than just mindset. It requires basic needs being met. When everyone has clean water, safe shelter, nourishing food, renewable energy, community and education, then no one is forced into relationships of dependency out of fear or survival. Only then can we enter business partnerships, marriages, and communities freely and consciously.

The Female Revolution: From Domestic Workers to Partnership Sovereignty

For centuries, women were the unpaid domestic workers of civilization — the quiet architects of family life whose labor built nations but rarely earned recognition. Their work was vital, yet invisible. In most of history, a woman's survival depended upon marriage, and marriage itself functioned as an economic contract disguised as romance. She could not open a bank account, own land, or vote. Her name disappeared into her husband's, and her livelihood was secured only through obedience and endurance.

But history has a way of stirring even the deepest silences. During World War II, when men left for the frontlines, women stepped into the factories, offices, and laboratories of the world. They built ships, airplanes, and communications systems that sustained entire economies. They proved that competence, intelligence, and ingenuity were not gendered qualities but human ones. And when the war ended, though they were asked to return quietly to their kitchens, something irreversible had awakened. Women had tasted their own sovereignty — and the world would never again fit back into the old mold.

The decades that followed birthed one of humanity's most transformative revolutions — not waged with guns or flags, but with voices, pens, and unyielding courage. Women organized for fair wages, education, and reproductive rights, and for the ability to choose love instead of depend upon it. They demanded a seat at the table — and then built their own tables when none were offered.

A Case Study: Iceland's Day Off

On October 24, 1975, nearly 90% of Icelandic women did something revolutionary. They stopped working — not just in offices or factories, but in their homes, kitchens, and schools. They called it a "Women's Day Off," and for one remarkable day, the country ground to a halt. Offices closed. Flights were canceled. Fathers brought their children to work because daycares were empty. The sound of silence — the sound of unpaid labor withdrawn — echoed across the island.

Their message was simple: *If women stop, society stops.*

This peaceful, united act reshaped an entire nation's consciousness. The following year, Iceland passed its first Gender Equality Act, and only five years later, the country elected Vigdís Finnbogadóttir, the world's first democratically elected female president. The women of Iceland proved that the invisible labor of love and care is not just sentimental — it is structural. It holds civilization together.

Their revolution was not about domination or reversal of roles — it was about revelation. By refusing to participate in a system that undervalued them, they reminded the world of an eternal truth: that the health of any society depends not on who controls it, but on how well it honors those who sustain it.

Redefining Partnership and Power

Today, that revolution continues to unfold. Across the world, women are opting out of dependency-based marriage models and redefining partnership as mutual empowerment rather than economic necessity. They are choosing lives that balance love with freedom, purpose with passion, and care with autonomy.

This is not a revolt against men; it is a homecoming to wholeness. When women reclaim their power, men are liberated too — from the burden of domination, from the expectation to control, and from the belief that love is ownership. Together, we are learning that true partnership is not built on dependence but on dignity.

The feminine revolution is not a war for supremacy. It is a remembrance — of balance, reciprocity, and the natural harmony between the masculine and the feminine. It is a radical departure from domination culture to want to heal the human family in hopes that it may be free and reach its highest potential.

"The world of humanity is possessed of two wings: the male and the female. So long as these two wings are not equivalent in strength, the bird will not fly."

–Abdu'l-Baha, the Baha'i Faith

CHAPTER 10

HOW TO RECLAIM DIGNITY FROM DEPENDENCE

"Freedom is the soul of every great creation."
— Rabindranath Tagore

Dependence is the quiet addiction of modern life. We depend on corporations to feed us, governments to guide us, jobs to validate us, and systems we neither understand nor control to sustain us. We are, in essence, outsourcing our sovereignty.

To reclaim dignity, we must re-member—literally *put back together*—our capacity to meet our own needs, to create beauty, and to live in right relationship with one another and the Earth.
Freedom does not begin with protest. It begins with practice.

Here's how we can begin.

1. Reclaiming the Basics of Sovereignty
Food

- **Start a garden**, no matter how small. A windowsill herb garden or balcony tomato plant reconnects us to nourishment that is ours.
- **Join or start a local food co-op.** Pooling community resources to buy directly from local farmers bypasses centralized supply chains.
- **Learn food preservation.** Canning, fermenting, and drying food reawakens generational skills that reduce dependency on constant consumption.
- **Support regenerative farms.** Choose farmers who rebuild soil, sequester carbon, and treat land as sacred, not as an extractive asset.

Every seed planted is an act of quiet rebellion against dependence.

Water

- **Catchment systems.** Where laws allow, install rain barrels or tanks. It's both practical and symbolic: the sky can provide.
- **Atmospheric water generators (AWGs).** New technology literally pulls drinking water from thin air, liberating homes and villages from centralized supply.
- **Protect local watersheds.** Join restoration efforts—plant native trees along stream banks, reduce chemical use, and monitor water quality.

Clean water is not a commodity; it's a birthright. Reclaiming it restores both ecological and personal dignity.

Energy

- **Go solar.** Even a single panel for lighting or charging devices is a start.
- **Share resources.** Neighborhood micro-grids can power multiple homes, turning dependency into interdependence.
- **Shift habits.** Energy sovereignty begins with awareness—turning off unused lights, cooking with the sun, or walking instead of driving.

Each watt we generate ourselves is a vote for autonomy.

2. Reclaiming the Soul of Work
Small Steps

- **Turn your skill into a service.** Whether it's baking, repairing, writing, or teaching, start offering it locally or online.
- **Barter and trade.** Exchange your expertise for someone else's instead of always buying.
- **Work fewer hours in jobs that drain you** and more hours in activities that build something real. Even part-time self-employment begins to dissolve dependence.

Larger Shifts

- **Form micro-enterprises.** Partner with neighbors to produce goods, crafts, or food for local sale.
- **Launch a cooperative.** Worker-owned businesses like *Mondragon* in Spain or *Equal Exchange* in the U.S. prove that shared ownership scales.
- **Transition to local production.** From community bakeries to repair cafés, every local creation restores human-scale dignity to labor.

Work that honors life restores the worker.

3. Reclaiming Financial Freedom
Small Steps

- **Move money locally.** Shift some savings to a local credit union or community bank that reinvests in your region.
- **Buy less, create more.** Minimalism isn't deprivation—it's the art of owning what supports your wholeness.
- **Invest in relationships, not returns.** The best "interest" you'll ever earn is mutual trust.

Larger Shifts

- **Cooperative investment funds.** Communities can pool resources to finance local energy, housing, and food projects.
- **Local currencies and time banks.** Hours and skills can circulate as alternative economies, like the *BerkShares* in Massachusetts or *Kōkua Credits* in Hawaii.
- **Land trusts and co-housing.** Shared ownership structures prevent speculation and ensure permanent affordability.

When money circulates in circles of trust, wealth becomes wellbeing.

4. Reclaiming Health and Healing
Small Steps

- **Cook real food.** Every meal made from scratch is an act of self-care and sovereignty.
- **Move naturally.** Walk, stretch, dance, swim—reclaim movement from machines. Even the way we move has been influenced by our culture. We think that swimming is about distance or speed and it follows a straight line. Running on a tread mill is artificial and totally devoid of connection to nature. Lifting weights is about counting numbers and moving in straight lines. "No pain, no gain!" It's time to question everything.
- **Cultivate emotional resilience.** Practice mindfulness, journaling, or time in nature instead of medicating disconnection.

Larger Shifts

- **Community care networks.** Health co-ops and mutual aid groups lower costs and strengthen belonging.
- **Holistic wellness hubs.** Many small towns now host shared spaces for acupuncture, yoga, herbalism, and counseling— healing as community ritual, not commodity.

When we heal ourselves, we heal the culture of dependence that profits from our illness.

5. Reclaiming Community and Meaning
Small Steps

- **Host gatherings.** Shared meals, music nights, or storytelling circles remind us we are richer together.
- **Skill-sharing events.** Exchange know-how: composting, carpentry, sewing, coding.
- **Local storytelling.** Collect your elders' wisdom before it disappears; culture is our most endangered resource.

Larger Shifts

- **Community land trusts and eco-villages.** Shared ownership models anchor land in trust for future generations.
- **Local governance.** Form councils or assemblies where decisions are made by consensus, not by remote authority.
- **Regenerative education.** Teach children not how to compete but how to collaborate.

Connection is the antidote to domination.

6. The Inner Work of Reclaiming Dignity

Dependence is not only economic—it is psychological. To reclaim dignity, we must confront the internalized belief that we are powerless, replaceable, or incapable of meeting our own needs.

This begins with awareness:

- **Gratitude practice** trains the mind to recognize abundance rather than lack.
- **Creative expression** reconnects us with our generative power.
- **Meditation and mythic storytelling** remind us who we are beyond the roles society assigns.

Gandhi's true revolution was not political—it was *spiritual.* He taught that to change the world, we must first change our relationship to fear and dependence within.

Freedom begins in the heart before it manifests in the world.

7. The Path Forward: A New Kind of Prosperity

Dignity is not granted by systems; it is cultivated by souls. To reclaim it, we do not need permission, policies, or revolutions. We simply need to remember that our worth is not measured by our wage.

Each small act of sovereignty—each seed planted, loaf baked, neighbor helped, and story told—loosens the grip of dependence and strengthens the web of life.

The future will not be built by giants. It will be built by gardeners, artisans, healers, and dreamers who refuse to sell their souls for survival. And when enough of us choose creation over compliance, the economy of domination will quietly collapse—replaced by the economy of care.

CHAPTER 11
DECENTRALIZATION AS LIBERATION

Our dependence on centralized systems—power grids, sewage, water lines—keeps us trapped. We rely on the government or private industry to tell us where we can build our homes based on where these centralized services can reach, and we pay taxes to keep the huge infrastructure up to date. But decentralization can liberate us.

Example: On the Big Island of Hawai'i (where I live), $1 billion is needed to upgrade our current central wastewater plants and it will take another billion to bring 90% of our houses up to par with septic tanks. These plants already dump raw sewage into the ocean when "king tides" or heavy rains overwhelm them. The septic systems are also not infallible, and the sewage still may need to be pumped out and processed by the outdated plants at some point.

What if we decentralized our wastewater systems to process our waste one flush at a time instead. Imagine a toilet that (like a Lectrasan on a boat) simply macerated and electrified waste when you flushed. Done! Now, the benign gray water could flow into the Earth without worry of disease or contamination. No chemicals necessary. If we replaced about 115,000 toilets on our island with a processing unit (at an estimated cost of $230 million total) we would save almost 90% of the $2 billion needed to revamp the old systems.

Since the compact processing unit requires some electricity, let's use that savings to provide solar power to all 90,000 homes (at an estimated cost of $1.8 billion). That will save over $3.2 billion in electric bills for households over the next 25 years. That's a fraction of the centralized plan.

While we're at it, let's give every household, workplace and school its own clean drinking water – a fresh water spring in every home. It's called an atmospheric water generator and makes plenty of fresh drinking water for a family every day right out of thin air. They cost about $900 (an estimated total cost of $89 million) right now. That would eliminate the cost to our children of lead poisoning, a chronic problem caused by the water fixtures at Hawaii's schools. 2% of the children in Hawaii schools reportedly tested positive for lead poisoning – that's over 3,000 children state wide (statistically). It is estimated that the special needs cost of the healthcare for each child with lead poisoning can be $50,000 per year or $150 million per year. It's sad to even discuss lead poisoning as an issue in 2025 or to assign it a monetary value that in no way compensates for the child's permanent damage. Needless to say, it's a much greater cost than providing each family their own source of fresh, clean water.

Finally, off the grid living would be safe and comfortable with amenities and technologies such as those described above. That means we could live just about anywhere in Hawaii, lowering the price of land and housing to an affordable level. That means Hawaiians could afford to stay in Hawaii and transplants could move here without adding much more stress to the infrastucture.

This is not just about Hawai'i. It's a metaphor. Decentralization reduces vulnerability, increases sovereignty, and returns power to the people. Sustainability doesn't mean giving up comfort—it means giving up dependence. Here's a real-world example, Puerto Rico.

Puerto Rico — From Collapse to Decentralized Resilience

When Hurricane Maria struck Puerto Rico in 2017, the island became a mirror for the vulnerability of centralized systems. Within hours, the entire electrical grid failed. Roads became impassable, hospitals went dark, and communication collapsed. In the aftermath, analysts said the disaster had "set Puerto Rico back by twenty-six years." The official recovery plan estimated more than $130 billion would be needed to rebuild essential infrastructure — a task projected to take well over a decade.

But even as reconstruction began, climate scientists warned: storms of Maria's magnitude were no longer "once-in-a-century." Another major hurricane could strike again within a decade. The math was unforgiving. Rebuilding the same fragile, centralized system was not resilience — it was roulette.

And so, quietly, a new story began.

Across Puerto Rico, citizens, cooperatives, and local leaders started imagining an energy system that could survive the next storm. Instead of one massive, brittle grid dependent on imported fossil fuels, they began building many small, interlinked systems powered by the sun and wind. In mountain towns like Adjuntas, community solar microgrids now light homes and businesses even when the main grid fails. Cooperativas Hidroeléctricas de la Montaña combine hydro and solar generation to serve rural families previously left for last in every recovery cycle.

At the national level, the transformation is accelerating. The Puerto Rico Energy Resilience Fund — administered by the U.S. Department of Energy — is investing over a billion dollars to deploy rooftop solar and battery storage across vulnerable communities. The island's Grid Modernization Plan calls for a distributed network of renewable microgrids capable of "islanding" during storms — each one small enough to be self-healing, yet interconnected enough to share power when others go down.

The shift is not complete. As of 2025, large portions of the central grid remain under repair, and bureaucratic delays still slow federal funding. But the cultural shift — from dependency to local autonomy — is unmistakable. Power is no longer imagined only as something that flows *from above*, but something that rises *from within*. Each solar rooftop, each battery bank, each community-owned grid node becomes an act of sovereignty: people choosing to generate, store, and share their own lifeline.

Puerto Rico's evolving energy landscape offers a living metaphor for what decentralized resilience looks like. It is not chaos or fragmentation — it is diversity in service of survival. When one part of the system falls, others stand. When the grid fails, light still shines.

In this way, Puerto Rico is teaching the world what every civilization on a warming planet must soon learn: that resilience cannot be outsourced. It must be rooted where people live, woven into the fabric of daily life, and entrusted to the hands of those who have the most to lose — and the most to gain — from keeping the lights on when the storm arrives again.

CHAPTER 12
THE COURAGE TO LIVE BEYOND SURVIVAL

"You are not a drop in the ocean. You are the entire ocean, in a drop."
— Rumi

The Great Forgetting

From the moment we are born, we are taught to survive. To earn. To achieve. To compete. We are not taught to *remember*. We forget that before we were citizens, consumers, or even children of parents—we were souls. We came here for the adventure of being human: to taste, to touch, to love, to learn, to play in creation itself.

The Earth was never meant to be a battlefield for survival.
It was meant to be a living classroom and garden of wonder—a sacred playground where spirit experiences form. Domination culture begins in the forgetting of that truth. When we forget we are eternal, survival becomes our only religion.

The Shift from Fear to Faith

Fear says: *I must control life to stay alive.*
Faith whispers: *I am life, and life cannot die.*

This shift is not philosophical—it's visceral. When we remember that our soul existed long before this lifetime and will continue long after, our priorities reorder themselves. Suddenly, selling our integrity for safety makes no sense. Fear loses its grip when death itself is no longer the enemy.

Every act of courage—whether speaking truth, quitting a soulless job, or planting a garden instead of buying plastic food—is a declaration of faith in life's continuity. It is how we begin to live from eternity rather than anxiety.

Living in Alignment with the Soul

To live soul-first is to treat each choice as sacred.
Ask not, "Will this make me secure?" but, "Will this make me whole?"

- **Integrity over income.** If a paycheck requires you to betray your values, it costs too much.
- **Creativity over conformity.** Your unique expression is how spirit evolves through you.
- **Joy over justification.** Pleasure is not indulgence—it is alignment with the current of life.

When we live this way, survival becomes the *side effect* of authenticity, not its opposite.

The Eternal Perspective

Our souls have worn thousands of bodies, played countless roles—rich and poor, straight and gay, male and female. Each incarnation offers a new vantage point from which to remember the same truth: **Love is the only thing that endures.**

Seen from that eternal view, every challenge becomes curriculum. Fear is the teacher that points us back to trust. Loss is the fire that refines what cannot be lost. Death is simply the doorway home.

The courage to live one's truth—even if it costs comfort or status— comes from knowing that the game of survival was never the goal.

Practicing Spiritual Sovereignty

Reclaiming dignity from dependence isn't just about decentralizing economies—it's about decentralizing *fear*.

Here are simple practices that restore spiritual remembrance:

1. **Begin each day with the bigger picture.**
   Say aloud: *I am a soul, eternal and safe. Today I will play, learn, and create in harmony with life.*

2. **End each day in gratitude.**
   List three moments of connection—to nature, to another soul, to your own joy.
3. **Walk barefoot on the earth.**
   Remember your body is made of the same minerals, water, and starlight as the planet itself.
4. **Create something daily.**
   Art, music, food, kindness—creation is the soul's proof of existence.
5. **Release the illusion of control.**
   Practice letting life surprise you. The unknown is not the enemy—it's the adventure you came for.

The Return to Eden

The Garden of Eden was never lost—it was merely forgotten. It still blooms wherever we live in harmony with the living world and the truth of who we are. When we reclaim our spiritual identity, Earth reclaims her sacredness through us.

We are not here to escape the world; we are here to sanctify it—to make every act, from growing food to making love, a conversation between matter and spirit.

This remembrance is the ultimate liberation from domination culture: When we know we cannot die, no one can make us live in fear.

To refuse to sell our souls for survival is not reckless—it is reverent. It is to trust that the universe sustains those who live in truth, even if the old structures crumble around them. The soul's path is not about safety; it is about sovereign participation in creation. And once we remember that, dependence dissolves. What remains is belonging—to life itself.

CHAPTER 13
SPIRITUAL SOVEREIGNTY:
AS SEEN IN THE LIFE OF CHRIST

Jesus's life is, in many ways, the archetypal story of spiritual sovereignty
— of one who refused to sell his soul for survival or riches and lived
fully aligned with Divine truth, even when that choice cost him his life.

Here's how Christ's life demonstrates this principle:

He Refused to Be Governed by Fear

When tempted in the desert, Jesus was offered all the kingdoms of the
world if he would bow to domination — to power and control. He
refused. This was not just a moral stand; it was a demonstration that
true authority flows from within, not from external power structures.

He Lived as a Sovereign Soul in a System of Domination

Rome was the empire of empires — an economy of fear, taxation, and
hierarchy. Jesus moved freely through it without buying into its rules.
He healed without a license, taught without credentials, and associated
with those the system rejected — the poor, women, lepers, tax
collectors, and outcasts.

Every act of compassion was an act of rebellion against domination
culture. He demonstrated that *love itself* was the highest law — higher
than Caesar's authority, higher even than the rigid hierarchies of
religion.

He chose his battles wisely when political leaders tried to trap him in
regard to whether one should pay taxes. Jesus said "Render therefore
unto Caesar the things which are Caesar's . . ."

He Modeled a Cooperative Kingdom

Jesus described his vision not as an empire but as a "Kingdom of
Heaven" — a community built on love, service, and equality. In that
realm, the first are last, and the greatest are servants.

He gathered a circle of disciples — not soldiers — and taught them to share everything in common. The early Christian communities practiced this literally, pooling resources and ensuring that no one lacked what they needed (*Acts* 4:32–35).

This was not charity. It was trust-based interdependence — a prototype of a cooperative, regenerative society.

He Trusted in Divine Provision

Jesus lived without possessions, status, or guarantee of tomorrow. Yet he never acted from scarcity. He fed thousands with a few loaves and fishes — not as a magic trick, but as a demonstration that faith multiplies abundance.

> *"Consider the lilies of the field... they neither toil nor spin,*
> *yet your Father clothes them."* — Matthew 6:28

He invited us to live in that same trust: that when we align with love, life itself provides what we truly need. Lillies, by the way, are still rooted in the soil, enjoying their connection to earth, sun and rain, surrounded by nature. If Lillies had to work in a cubicle 40 hours/week, I have to wonder if they would feel our "toil."

He Faced Death Without Betraying His Soul

At the height of fear and coercion — trial, torture, crucifixion — he did not retaliate or conform. He forgave his oppressors, embodying the ultimate spiritual sovereignty: the power to choose love even when surrounded by hate.

In doing so, he shattered the illusion that survival is the highest goal. He showed that *eternal life* — the continuity of consciousness, truth, and love — is already within us.

The Resurrection: The Soul's Triumph Over Fear

The resurrection story is not only about physical life after death; it's the symbolic revelation that spirit cannot be dominated. No empire, no system, no cross can kill the truth of who we are. This is the deepest meaning of "refusing to sell the soul for survival" — to live so fully in integrity that even death becomes transformation, not defeat.

The Living Lesson

Jesus's entire ministry can be summed up as this invitation:

Remember who you are. Live as if you are eternal. Love as if you cannot lose.

He showed us that when we release fear of loss — reputation, wealth, status, or even life itself — we reclaim our Divine dignity. That is how the human spirit becomes indomitable.

CHAPTER 14
A VISION FOR THE FUTURE

Imagine a world where homes are off-grid sanctuaries of energy and water self-sufficiency. Where mortgage and rent are no more. Where people choose their careers and relationships not from fear, but from soul calling.

Cottage industries thrive. Artistry is valued. No one profits from another's exploitation. Instead, partnerships flourish, rooted in reciprocity.

This is not utopia. It is a real possibility—if we dare to reframe what being human can mean.

And to make it real, let us embrace a coherent philosophy for a generous economy of belonging to buoy us in times of spiritual amnesia.

THE GIFT WE'RE MEANT TO BE

We were born into a world that gives first.

The rain does not invoice the soil.
The tree does not demand payment for shade.
The serviceberry offers its sweetness freely,
not as a transaction,
but as a continuation of life.

Before money, before markets,
there was the gift—
and we were meant to be part of its circulation.

We Are Not Separate

There is no "I" without "we."
Our nervous systems are attuned to one another.
Our joy is not a zero-sum game.

66

Our survival is not a solo act.

The story of the separate self
was never our real story—
just a long forgetting.

We are threads in the web.
When we tug one, all feel it.
When we give, all grow.

Abundance Is Not Accumulation

To hoard is to interrupt the flow.
To give is to remember our place in the river of life.
Nature teaches this again and again:

The salmon feeds the forest.
The mushroom shares its sugars.
The bird plants the tree.

Let us build an economy
where generosity is strategy,
and where trust is the currency
that holds our wealth in common.

We Are Meant to Be Gifts

Not consumers, but contributors.
Not brands, but beings.
Not extractors, but expressions
of a living, breathing Earth.

Our hands were made for crafting,
our voices for singing,
our hearts for offering.

What the world needs is what lives in us—
our stories, our care, our courage, our creativity.

We are not burdens to society.
We are the medicine it has forgotten.

The Circle Is the Shape of Justice

No one left behind.
No one on top.

Power is not a ladder;
it is a fire we gather around,
passing warmth, passing wisdom.

A community of gifts
has no beggars and no kings—
only people who remember
that we belong to each other.

A New Economy Begins With Us

Let us design systems rooted in reciprocity,
where profit is measured in well-being,
and success means everyone eats,
everyone is safe,
everyone can sing their soul's song.

Let us build with our hands,
barter with our hearts,
and plant seeds not just in soil,
but in systems.

Closing Declaration

We are the gift we've been waiting for.

We carry ancient wisdom in our blood
and future solutions in our bones.

We remember.
We reweave.
We return.

We are the Gift We're Meant to Be.

Christ used parables or short stories to help humanity remember itself on a transpersonal level (beyond mere personality). Storytelling, especially mythic stories, bring their message home. The following story prefers to be told around the fire at night amongst those we want to call kin. This myth is "open source" meaning it came to me open hearted, and I share it as such – so that if it calls you to retell it, feel free to answer its call and add your own flair that it may continue to evolve.

STAR RIDER – A MYTHIC TALE

Not so long ago in a place no so far away, a young sailor lost his soul in the ocean. His soul was so heavy that it quickly sunk to the bottom of the abyss, thousands of miles deep below, and was probably buried in the mud and encrusted by barnacles by now.

Without a soul, he went through his daily chores aboard ship without complaining, just going through the motions. He kept his head down and never spoke hoping the cruel captain wouldn't notice him. Ports didn't interest the sailor, and he hardly noticed the moon most nights.

The sailor's main job was to swab the dirty decks of the wooden sailing ship so they wouldn't smell of fish. In exchange for his labor, he would receive a small ration of food and water which was limited aboard ship because the crew had to make it stretch across long passages. His only glimmer of hope were the stars. He sometimes climbed to the top of the mast at night and wondered how he might hop on one while it shot across the sky to freedom.

After a strong storm hit the ship, some of the food rations had washed overboard, not leaving enough for all the crew to reach their destination. Stress levels rose, the captain became even more cruel making everyone work even harder with less food. When the sailor caught a cold and was too weak to work at all, he was made to the walk the plank. That's how all rule-breakers were punished, and rules were rules.

As he teetered on the edge of the plank, he was surprised that he didn't seem to care if he lived or died that night. Instead of feeling betrayed by his crew after years of faithful service, he felt nothing. So, he jumped from the plank into the cold ocean. Instead of struggling, the souless sailor simply allowed the water to embrace him.

He began to float as he lay on his back just as he had done as a boy when he used to dream of being crew on a sailing ship. He remembered how free he used to feel back then. His arms outstretched, he relaxed and felt the rhythmic lapping of the gentle waves against his skin.

He could taste the salt of the sea in his mouth and it reminded him of the tears that used to run down his hot checks so long ago. He remembered how he would play with the ocean waves as a boy running along her shores as they crashed on the beach trying to catch his feet. He remembered how the wind used to play with his hair, tusseling it in all sorts of new styles to make him laugh.

Then he looked up. He never remembered seeing such a huge full moon before. It towered in gold light above him allowing him to see for miles in the night. The old ship was nowhere in sight.

All alone, floating under the moon, he remembered that when he had a soul, he laughed more, sang sea shanties, and had more stories to tell – the kind of stories that used to touch people's hearts.

Floating under the moon, he felt a ripple, and then some bubbles tickle his back as they burst on the surface. He realized he wasn't alone after all, and fear immediately washed over him. He thought he might be swallowed by a whale or wrapped up for dinner by a giant squid or eaten for appetizers by a school of sharks.

As he turned over to face his fate, he opened his eyes under water to discover a shimmering tail and the face of a woman looking at him curiously. A mermaid had come to admire the full moon with the sailor. She knew that full moons are always more fun when shared with a friend.

"Aloha, I'm Vyana" said the mermaid. "Who are you?"

I'm just a sailor who has lost his soul," he replied.

"Do you remember where you left it," she asked.

"Oh, yes, I flung it into the sea long ago on a night just like this," he said.

"Why would you throw your soul away?" asked the Vyana curiously.

"I was a sailor on a ship called the Rat Race. Our cruel captain treated the crew like he owned us. We all wanted to escape, but the by the time we heard the stories about the loathsome deaths that awaited us if we were to jump ship, we were to afraid to do anything. To make things worse, we had to pretend to be happy and smile whenever he was near.

Well, my soul would have nothing to do with that and it kept rebelling! A rebel on a ship is forced to walk the plank, so I finally had to choose between my soul and my survival.

After many a sleepless night and much inner turmoil, I finally flung my soul into the sea when no one was looking. I haven't felt much of anything since then. No joy, no laughter, no real friends – but hey, I survived."

"So what are you doing out here floating alone under the moon?" asked the mermaid.

"I guess my fate will be like my soul. I'll probably sink into the muck at the bottom of the sea and be forgotten," said the sailor.

"Hmm. Have you thought about singing it to you?" she asked.

"What do you mean?" said the sailor.

"Well whenever I feel sad or alone, singing makes me feel better."

"I haven't sung a song in years," said the sailor. "What would I sing? I've forgotten any songs."

"Perfect!" said the mermaid. "New songs are the best. You just have to make one up."

"How do I do that?" asked the sailor.

"You open your mouth, take a deep breath and let the song fall out. It doesn't work if you try too hard or if you care what anyone else thinks," explained the mermaid.

"How will I know what magic words to use to call my soul back?" asked the sailor.

"That's the magic part. If you don't think about it, the words just come – like magic," replied the mermaid.

"Like this. Watch me." She floated on her back facing the moon, relaxed into the gentle waves and began to make sounds that felt like they came from the bottom of her tail and travelled an all the way up and out the top of her head. Having warmed up that way, melodies began to flow from the mermaid that felt like home to the sailor, even though it was in a language he had never heard before. Normally a mermaid song would cause a sailor to fall in love, but even the most enchanting song has nowhere to land if a man has no soul.

"Now you try!" said the mermaid.

So, the sailor, mesmerized by the harmonic waves that now flooded his body decided to give it a try. Laying on his back, surrendered to the salty waters' embrace and with the full moon pulling him in, he let out a CROAK that scared even himself.

The mermaid seemed tickled and began laughing and cheering at the sailor's first song. She said, "Perfect! We all croak the first time. You're right on track. Now this time you won't be so self-conscious."

And so. . . the Sailor summoned his courage and surrendered to the many strange and forlorn sounds of longing that a soulless man drifting on the sea alone might make.

But just as the mermaid expected, magic happened. An entire school of flying fish jumped over the sailor creating such a stir that the sailor almost jumped out of his skin.

The mermaid laughed and said, "The ocean is filled with so many fish and friends that we are never really alone. If you look closely, you'll see that there are more creatures than water, especially at night when the moon is full!"

"But I'm afraid," exclaimed the sailor. "What if one of those creatures means to hurt me?"

"You're right! Danger lurks everywhere," said the mermaid. 'That's why you hardly ever see a mermaid. Most of us are hiding out in remote sandy coves, unknown caves and under waterfalls – to steer clear of men like your cruel captain. If more humans were kind like you, then we would come out to play more. Most humans are taught to be afraid of mermaids, fairies and other magical creatures they don't understand yet."

"How can I understand anyone else if I don't have a soul?" asked the exasperated sailor.

"Ah yes, the soul song," remembered the mermaid. "While you were singing, your soul broke free of the mud and crusties. Naturally, it began to float toward the surface.

That's when the dolphins founded it and playing with it awakened its joy.

Then the jellyfish gently lifted it up without much effort at all.

A friendly turtle carried it on its back to bring it closer to you.

Finally, the flying fish came by to create enough stir to awaken you to its presence. All you have to do is reach out and give your soul a big hug. It has missed you more than you know."

And so he did. The sailor hugged his soul close and promised never to lose it again. More salty tears were added to the ocean that night. His soul began to hum from deep inside a warm and playful melody which made him float even more under the full light of the moon.

The mermaid took the sailor's hand and floating under the starry sky, used her powerful tail to propel them to shore. The bioluminescence glowed around them as dolphins jumped their wake silhouetted by the moon. As they felt the soft sand below them, the mermaid's tail became legs and they were greeted by two young women who seemed to know they were coming. The women wrapped them both in flowing robes of white and hung sweet smelling flowers about their necks.

The tropical island on which they landed was inhabited by a village of happy people who welcomed them to their monthly festival – a full moon celebration. This was the moon that brought them the tides and lit their night sky. This was the moon that told the people when to pull weeds and when to plant their gardens creating plenty of food for all. The people's faces shined just like the moon, apparently fulfilled by joy they could not contain. The joy was like a river of contagious laughter in the shimmer of all the bling bling for sale at the night market. Everyone had a booth – everyone seemed to be an artist of some kind. Every booth seemed to have its own color, geometry and music, creating a kaleidoscope of creative expression – giving the market a dance of its own.

First they stopped at the booth fills with handwoven fabrics died in a rainbow of colors and prints. They were asked to choose their favorite color at that moment and were each gifted a light wrap that hung over their white robes. The mermaid chose peacock blue like the deepest ocean, and the sailor chose silver and gold woven together. The tailor approved of their color choices and said it would highlight their auras. Before the sailor could even ask what an aura was, the mermaid was dragging him to the next booth where a master blender was making essential oils.

75

She was drawn there by the smell of linden blossom that infused the entire bazaar with such sweetness that she remembered the blend her mother had gifted her on her 16th birthday. It was a signature blend just for her and her mother had called it "sovereignty." The smell transported her to feel her mother's embrace – the smell of homecoming. Meanwhile, the master blender had taken an interest in the sailor because he still smelled like fish, and recommended they start their evening at the spa booth, have something to eat and return to him for special blend of essential oils that would honor the sailor.

The Sailor had never been to a spa. They began at the waterfall where the fresh water warmed by the volcano above would flow down to several pools. Each pool had a variety of floating flowers, and incense to clear the heart and mind as well as the body. Small oil lamps made out of seashells and nut oil lit the path. Mermaid sisters came to the spa often to braid each other's hair not just because the gentle braiding felt wonderful, but because it symbolized the weaving of their lives together. They would also exchange pearls with each other, each one representing a dear friend or family member, and each one knotted onto their string of pearls to travel home with them.

As was the custom for any guest arriving from a journey, the lomi lomi massage started with a sacred chant and coconut oil on their feet. Soon, they were both slathered from head to toe and both and may have even fallen asleep for a moment. The sailor didn't remember the last time he had been so lavished. The sailor's body didn't lie. It was covered with scars of battles gone by. It was aching from years of labor and soulless repetition. The lomi lomi provider could feel that the soul had only recently returned, and so lovingly stitched it back together with the sailor's body. This is the kind of stitching that one learns from a grandmother who learned it from her grandmother.

Finally, the sailor and the mermaid emerged from the spa, now glowing like the other villagers, and caught a whiff of an essential oil they had never smelled before. Returning to essential oil booth, the blending master proceeded to anoint the sailor with a blend he called sky dreamer. The sailor couldn't make out what was in this magic elixir, but it made him think of cypress and black spruce growing tall and strong toward the sky.

Then Vyana noticed the smell of warm cinnamon coming from a booth that served simple dishes with heart-warming flavors. She sipped hot chocolate made with nutmeg and coconut milk while the sailor enjoyed baked sweet potato wedges. Fruits of every kind, most of which the sailor had never heard of were abundantly sampled.

The lively music that surrounded the festival and the happy chatter that peppered it were welcome after so many years aboard ship. Booths of every kind invited them in to taste their spices, to collect seashells, and to wear their jewelry. Small paintings on mulberry bark and poetry from wise ones were shared freely.

The island seemed to thrive on the novelty of art and on the refinement of each artist who would arrive at the festival each full moon with something new for all to experience. The mermaid particularly enjoyed the handy belts woven out of various seaweeds. Carrying treasure with her was always tricky since mermaid tails never have pockets.

The entire festival seemed to move in spirals with the dance floor as the center, and no one seemed to be in charge. It all seemed to flow together like one synchronized flock of colorful birds. Such prosperity was never a possibility where the sailor came from – the land of mere survival.

The poetry booth took great interest in the sailor's story of how he sang his soul back and asked him if his soul had a name. He had never thought of that before. Vyana reminded him not to think about it, but to ask his soul. His soul will certainly know. His soul had been waiting patiently for this moment and immediately burst out the name "Astradazar, star rider." When he spoke this name, a hush fell over the festival and the music stopped. Everyone froze staring at the sailor who was just as surprised as everyone else.

An old woman with a tall staff emerged from the whispering villagers and walked toward the sailor. Her hair silver and long, but braided with black feathers. Her cloak simple white with ancient symbols painted on it. She looked up toward the moon, outstretched her hands and slowly but powerfully announced his soul's name, "A – Stra – Da –Zar."

As she spoke, a cloud crossed the face of the moon and rain drops began to fall to the ground. The villagers quickly closed up their booths, protected their art, and emptied the dance floor.

The old woman approached the sailor and held his gaze for some time. Her eyes were blue like the sea, and the rain seemed not to bother her.

"What was your favorite booth, Astradazar?" asked the old woman.

Most of all, he loved the feel of the soft leather bindings on the handmade paper books that had no words on them. He had never learned to read, so he had been embarrassed to pick up a book before, for fear of someone finding out. These empty books made him feel free and unlimited – just hundreds of blank pages waiting for a story. He said, "the book binder."

"And so, you are welcome storyteller. You carry stories of a lifetime of adventures from your travels aboard a sailing ship which will be greatly valued by our village. You may apprentice with our book binder who will teach you to read and write if it is your wish. I will teach you to remember the many adventures you have forgotten long before you came to be a sailor. You are not just any star rider -- you are Astradazar."

She continued, "We have heard stories of your star travels since the beginning. Our village will be blessed by your adventures of many star systems. I'm so happy the moon drew you to us!

Now, let me show you both to our extra homes where visitors stay until we help them build their own. Your custom home design will be informed from your soul-directed knowing -- geometries, colors and frequencies -- and if memory serves you well, you'll soon be off on another galactic adventure as one of our favorite solar system bards."

As they entered their sleeping domes made mostly of windows, amidst the scent of night-blooming jasmine and oranges, Astradazar turned around to quietly ask the old woman, "But what if I can't remember?"

She replied, "Have a little faith in the magic that you carry. If you had the courage to sing your soul back to you, then Memnos will help you remember who you really are."

"What is Memnos?" he asked.

"I'll show you soon. For now, rest and awaken to a new dream." The old woman shut the door, and everyone fell into a deep sleep.

When the sun arose, a breeze came through the open windows, and birds sang the village awake. Everyone seemed abuzz with excitement about the mysterious landing of the famous star-rider, Astradazar, in their little village.

There were no clocks in the village, so it's hard to say what time breakfast began as Mermaid Vyana and her star rider friend walked down the street arm in arm toward the wafting smell of cocoa and coffee. Both beans were abundant on this tropical island, and the village liked to mix them. This was the village where mochas were born and why the village was known to be cheerful and inviting. They often added white foam on top of the coffee to make it look like an ocean wave. In fact the name of the island was Mochaccino.

Wherever they stopped, whether in a coffee shop, a bookstore or an art studio, Vyana noticed that one tag line kept appearing: "Let us surprise and delight you!" The menus were full of surprises and shop owners prided themselves on delighting their guests. For example, one coffee shop gave away free coffee to those who came in dancing. Another shop featured unexpected serenades at your table, and the clothing store was completely empty with a sign that read, "Less is more!"

The tag line caught on after a fortune cookie washed up on shore with a fortune inside. It said, "Surprises and Delights await! Collect the magical moments." Everyone wanted their neighbor to feel that THEY were the one the cookie came for, so they all set out to make the fortune true – and they've been collecting evidence to that effect for so long, they've forgotten that THEY are the magic behind the fortune. The whole town just thinks its lucky.

When they sat down outside in the sun at a small table in front of the cocoa shop, they asked the owner where the old woman with silver hair might be found. The owner replied, "Which one – we have several wise women – and they all live in solitude at various edges of the village. What's her name?" Astradazar flushed, embarrassed that he had never asked his hostess for HER name. "What color were her eyes?" asked the shop owner. Astradazar had looked into her eyes intently last night, but he could not recall what color they were. "Well, no awareness prize for you!" joked Vyana.

The shop owner pulled up a chair and in a whisper, leaned over the table to say, "You know, we're all single in this small village. We all enjoy dating, and so, we have all learned to ask a lot more questions. It's simple, if we don't ask questions, we won't get to know everyone. We like to find out what kind of artist everyone is, and we like to help each other shine. Try it out! Who is this beautiful mermaid at your table?" he asked as he walked back to the kitchen to prepare their drinks.

And so Mermaid Vyana and Astradazar each took turns asking each other questions while sipping mochaccinos. They laughed as time flew by like shooting stars and they ended up ordering lunch as the owner played romantic music knowing they would never forget their first date at the Mochaccino Meet Up Café with Xavier, the owner, and his cat Malfi weaving between their legs.

Feeling more alive than ever, the only other thing Astradazar remembered about his silver-haired hostess was that he must introduce himself to the book binder and become his apprentice. Then he too would be able to read fortune cookies. Astradazar settled in to learning from Tanner, who was more than happy to have an apprentice. Tanner loved bookbinding and papermaking more than anything. He too had been an apprentice once. Tanner's love for words showed, and his words rang true. Astadazar noticed that true words seemed weightier than others – and dreamed of writing a poem for Vyana one day.

Mermaid Vyana spent her days in the sea and freshening up at the spa each evening before dinner with Astradazar where they would ask each other questions and try different restaurants. The village chefs quickly learned everyone's favorite dishes and added an extra something to surprise and delight. Vyana loved lobster and Astradazar was fond of cheese fondue. Their romance grew slowly as neither wanted to hasten a single moment.

At the next full moon festival, Astradazar's soul now fully inhabited his body, and his face shone as brightly as everyone else. He asked Vyana for every slow dance that night. Neither said anything, since there were no more questions left in the world that they hadn't asked. Under the moon, cheek to cheek, their lips met. The heart of mochaccino beat a little faster that night. He had almost forgot about the old woman with silver hair, but Vyana hadn't.

The next morning, Astradazar celebrated writing his first poem and reading it to Vyana at breakfast. The world looked different to him now – everything had meaning – rather than just scribbles on a menu – he could READ! He felt invincible, and couldn't wait to find the old woman with silver hair who would introduce him to Memnos that he might remember who he REALLY was as a star rider.

He asked Vyana to help him find the old woman that had greeted them that first night. She agreed. They asked the villagers to tell them about the seven old women who lived in solitude on the outskirts. They were seven sisters named: Maia, Electra, Taygete, Celaeno, Alcyone, Sterope and Merope. All were ancient daughters of an Oceanic Goddess, Pleione, who had founded this village over a thousand years ago. The villagers said that the sisters only came out at night, especially for festivals or to shine lights on the ocean and steer ships clear of the reef. They liked the night best because they could see all the brightest stars and they loved the quiet as the village slept. Their prayers were for wisdom and prosperity. Most of all, the sisters seemed to be the glue that held everyone together when a conflict arose. If anyone could help Astradazar remember his star-riding days, it would be these ancient sisters.

The villagers suggested that Astradazar learn as much as possible about his hostess and not arrive at her home empty handed. He should make her a gift. First he had to figure out which of the seven sisters he had met the first night under the full moon. He discovered from the village stories that each sister had a familiar, like a cat, a hawk, a wolf or a fox, and the like. They never went anywhere without their familiars except Merope who stopped taking her water dragon to festivals after it scared some of the children. Since the silver-haired woman he met at the festival did not have a familiar with her, it could only have been Merope.

He also remembered something blue about Merope, maybe it was her eyes. So he bound a dark blue leather book for her and embossed a water dragon design on the front. He made one for himself as well, since he knew he would need something in which to write his own memories as they returned.

On a clear bright evening, Astradazar set out to the home of Merope with his gift. Vyana wrapped a warm cloak around him and said, "This is YOUR journey, and you should visit Merope alone." He climbed up the volcano to a height that would allow him to see the entire layout of the village and hopefully pinpoint where Merope lived. As he looked down on the village at night, he saw the glow of golden lamp lights from many windows, and unexpectedly noticed 7 blue lights, all located in the outskirts of the town. The blue lights formed a familiar shape. He had seen this same configuration of blue light looking up at night from the ships deck. The sailors called this star cluster the Pleides. Of course, now, he could see the larger pattern – and remembered the names of the 7 stars that helped his ship to navigate were named after 7 sisters. Merope was one of the brightest at the bottom of the cluster. He knew exactly which house was hers.

Making his way down the mountain in the direction of Merope's home, he heard fresh water stream trickling down with him, and thirsty, he stopped to drink. It was dark, wet and slippery, and be found himself sliding down a deep ravine. Unharmed, he noticed he had landed in a drippy cave below the volcano. It wasn't dark, but he couldn't tell where the light was coming from. This was his favorite kind of adventure. As he made his way through the glowing wet cave, he came upon a glistening blue and purple dragon with lavender eyes. She was bigger than his old sailing ship even with her wings folded. He stood there not knowing what to do.

The dragon introduced herself. "Hello, I'm Memnos. We've been waiting for you."

Astradazar found his voice and asked how the dragon knew he was coming. Memnos replied that he'd been waiting for this moment for over a thousand years. The dragon went on, "You see, you share the same mother as Merope and her 6 sisters. Your mother's name was Pleione, which means plenty or sailor. Your home stars are the Pleides, and you are a star-rider. That means you love riding through the galaxy in search of adventure. Your sisters didn't hear from you for a great while and wondered where you were. They had heard that on Earth people often forget who they really are, and so they came here to find you.

"How do I break the amnesia and remember myself, Memnos?" he asked.

"I've brought just the thing -- water from our home stars. Water molecules are amazing – they never forget anything. If you drink this water from the Pleiades, it will reset your memory," she said as she handed Astradazar the sapphire blue bottle. He drank.

The water seemed more alive than ever. As it flowed down his throat, it ignited a bright blue light that felt exciting and expansive. As the water continued down, its light became green, warm and loving – the way he felt with Vyana. As the water continued down his front, it felt yellow in his center like it turned on the lights of his confidence and his purpose felt clear. As it continued, it turned red and felt like a passion to shoot to the sky. As it turned around and headed back up his spine, a violet light shot out of the top of his head that triggered all of his memories to return in a rush. The violet ray of remembrance of lifetimes of adventures among the stars and the space in between was clear like the water. He was beaming all over in every color.

That's when he heard it – "Memnos." He turned around to see the bright blue eyes of Merope again, the silver-haired woman who had met him that first night under the full moon. Tonight he met her as his sister, having drunk of Memnos -- the waters of remembrance. Tonight he was Astradazar and filled to the brim with stories to tell. His stories carried lifetimes of wisdom, poetry of the ages, technology beyond our wildest imagination, stories of truth and fulfillment that touched everyone deeply. The Pleidian family and Mermaid Vyana lived happily ever after in the little artist village and Astradazar began riding the stars again.

Closing Reflection: Remembering the Song of the Soul

When we leave the world of story and return to these pages, we may find ourselves changed—if only subtly. Something stirs. A memory, long buried. A truth not taught in school but known somewhere in the marrow of our bones.

Like the sailor, many of us have flung our souls into the depths just to survive. We've served under captains not of our choosing, followed rules that numbed our hearts, and traded dreams for rations of safety. We've kept our heads down in systems that punish rebellion and reward obedience. But there is another way.

The story of *Star Rider* is more than a tale—it's an invitation.

It reminds us that even if we feel numb, disconnected, or alone, we are never truly lost. Our souls are not gone. They are waiting. And sometimes, it takes just one moment of courage—a croaky song, a quiet float beneath the moon, a loving presence who believes in us—for our soul to rise again and remember.

This is the beginning of liberation: to reclaim the parts of ourselves we may have abandoned, not because we were weak, but because we were trying to stay alive in a system that forgot what life was for.

The village in the story is not a fantasy. It is a blueprint. It is what becomes possible when domination is replaced with cooperation, when production is replaced with artistry, when survival gives way to celebration.

You too have a song. A soul. A name the stars still remember.

Perhaps this is the moment to begin singing our souls home.

Inevitability

We must at some point set ourselves free, whether it is on the individual level of where we find a way to leave an abusive relationship, or overcome group mistreatment based on prejudice, or as a species that side-steps certain bacterial overgrowths, viral outbreaks, or one day repeats the cycle of abuse with beings from planets beyond our own. For if we fail in this freedom quest, then we will destroy ourselves and much of our planet in the process. For me, I will keep this vision alive, restore my soul and let my life be my message.

And for those who resonate with this philosophy, you may want to Declare your Inner Independence. Here is the Declaration I use to remind myself. You may want to create your own.

Declaration of Inner Independence
A Living Document for the Democracy of the Soul

I, a sovereign being in a living universe, hereby declare my independence from fear, domination, and deceit. I claim the freedom to live as love in action, to speak truth without hatred, and to remember my kinship with all life.

Article I — Sovereignty of the Soul

I govern myself through awareness, compassion, and conscience.
No external power shall define my worth or dictate my belonging.
I answer first to truth as I perceive it through the heart.
My thoughts, emotions, and actions are my domain, and I steward them with care.

Article II — Interdependence and Belonging

I belong to the Whole — not as property, but as participant.
I am one note in the great song of creation.
To honor my own freedom, I must also honor the freedom of others.
What harms another's liberty diminishes my own.

Article III — Nonviolence and Courage

I renounce cruelty, coercion, and deceit as tools of progress.
I choose the path of nonviolent truth-force (Satyagraha),
bearing witness with clarity and compassion.
Courage is my inheritance; love is my defense.

Article IV — Creative Responsibility

I am not a victim of systems; I am a creator of new ones.
Where domination builds walls, I plant gardens.

Where fear divides, I tell stories that remind us of our shared light.
My work, my art, my choices—all are votes for the world I wish to live in.

Article V — The Living Democracy

I affirm that democracy is more than law; it is a living covenant of
respect. Every voice is sacred. Every being, a universe.
I will listen before judging, invite dialogue before division,
and model cooperation as the highest form of leadership.

Article VI — The Regenerative Way

I commit to practices that restore life:
to give back what I take, to heal what I touch,
and to leave the Earth richer in beauty and wisdom than I found it.

Conclusion

Let this declaration be my compass in turbulent times.
May my life itself be my message:
That freedom and love are not opposites, but reflections of the same
living truth.

And if you want to bring this philosophy into your own community, here is a call to remembrance.

THE LIVING DEMOCRACY: A CALL TO REMEMBER

Prologue: The Great Remembering

We stand at a turning point in human history.
The old world—built on domination, extraction, and fear—has exhausted itself.
Its towers of hierarchy tremble, not because humanity has failed, but because we are remembering who we truly are.

Democracy, in its deepest sense, was never a government system—it was a covenant of the soul.
It is the living truth that *no one is free until all are free*, and that sovereignty without belonging is illusion.
We are not here to win power—we are here to *share it*.

I. The Principle of Living Sovereignty

True sovereignty begins within.
It is not the rule of one over another, but the mastery of the self in service to love.
A sovereign person is self-aware, self-governing, and self-responsible—and therefore cannot be ruled by tyranny, propaganda, or fear.

To live sovereignly is to choose awareness over obedience, conscience over compliance, and cooperation over control.

II. The Ecology of Democracy

A Living Democracy functions as a forest, not a factory.
It thrives on diversity, reciprocity, and rootedness.
Every person is a vital organism in this ecosystem of life—

unique, yet inseparable from the Whole.

We reject the notion that competition is the law of life.
We remember that *symbiosis* is nature's truer law.
Thus, we cultivate regenerative communities—
villages, circles, and cooperatives—
where freedom means participation, and equality means belonging.

III. The Courage of Cooperation

In times of division, cooperation is the most radical act.
It requires courage to listen across boundaries,
to replace judgment with curiosity,
to lead without dominating,
and to serve without disappearing.

Our task is not to destroy the old world, but to compost it—
to transform its decay into fertile soil for renewal.
We reclaim the word *power* as the capacity to create, not control.
And we wield it together.

IV. The Art of Moral Courage

The Living Democracy is held by conscience, not compliance.
When laws or leaders betray love, it is the moral duty of free beings to
disobey.
Civil courage is the quiet fire that protects the heart of democracy.
We resist hatred with humanity, lies with truth, and cruelty with creative
resistance.

As Gandhi taught: *"In a gentle way, you can shake the world."*

V. The Regenerative Covenant

We affirm a covenant with all beings—human and more-than-human.
Freedom without stewardship is consumption.

We are not rulers of the Earth; we are cells of her living body.
To heal democracy, we must also heal our relationship with the planet
that sustains it.

Therefore, we plant gardens instead of flags.
We build communities instead of empires.
We measure wealth in the abundance of life, not the accumulation of
power.

VI. The Practice of Belonging

The Living Democracy begins wherever two or more gather in truth.
It is practiced in kitchens, in tidepools, in town halls, and in hearts.
It is sustained not by armies, but by *agreements*—
by circles of trust, mutual care, and shared creativity.

Each of us is a microcosm of the greater whole.
When we live as sovereign souls in loving cooperation,
the world remembers its balance.

Epilogue: A Call to the Builders of Tomorrow

To all who can feel the world aching to be reborn:
the time for waiting is over.
Let us build the new civilization from the inside out—
from consciousness to community, from community to culture.

The Living Democracy is not a dream of the future.
It is the breath we share now,
the truth we speak now,
the love we live now.

And if you suffer on occasion from spiritual amnesia like me, you may find the following meditation helpful to recenter.

REMEMBRANCE MEDITATION:
The Courage to Live Beyond Survival

(This meditation can be read silently, spoken aloud, or recorded in your own voice with gentle background music — ocean waves, Tibetan bowls, or soft harp tones.)

Begin by finding a quiet place where you feel safe and comfortable.
Sit or lie down. Close your eyes.
Take a slow, deep breath in... and release it with a sigh.
Let the body begin to soften.
Let the earth hold you.

As you breathe, notice how your chest rises and falls —
how the air comes to you freely, without effort.
You are being breathed by Life itself.
You are safe. You are home.

Remembering Who You Are

Bring your awareness to your heart.
Imagine a soft golden light there, glowing warmly.
This light is the essence of your soul — ancient, wise, eternal.
It has been with you through every lifetime, every storm, every joy.

Whisper silently:

"I am a soul having a human experience.
I came here to love, to learn, to create, and to play."

Breathe this truth in...
and let it dissolve the old fear that you must earn your right to exist.
You already belong. You always have.

91

Releasing the Fear of Survival

Now imagine all the worries and obligations that have weighed on you:
bills, expectations, deadlines, judgments.
See them as small gray clouds floating around you.
With each breath, gently blow them away.

You do not need to carry them around with you.
They were never who you are.

Say softly:

"I release the anxiety of survival.
I choose to live in the truth that all is well with my soul."

Feel the light in your heart expand,
filling your whole chest, your whole body, until you are radiant.
Your spiritual integrity is your true security.

Reconnecting with the Living Earth

Now, imagine roots extending from your feet deep into the soil.
They reach down through the layers of rock and water,
until they touch the molten heart of the Earth.
You feel her pulse — slow, steady, loving.

Her energy rises through your roots,
through your legs, through your spine,
merging with the golden light of your soul.

Together, heaven and earth breathe you —
you are the bridge between spirit and matter.

Say within:

"I belong to the living Earth.
I am sustained by love, not fear."

The Eternal Perspective

Now, lift your awareness to the space above your head —
a vast night sky filled with stars.
Each star is one of your lifetimes,
each a spark of your infinite story.

From this higher view, you see that every challenge,
every loss, every triumph has been part of your soul's dance.
Nothing has ever been wasted.
Nothing has ever been lost.

Whisper:

"I am eternal.
This life is a single breath in the great song of existence."

And as you say these words, feel the immense relief of knowing
that nothing can truly go wrong in a universe made of love.

Returning as a Sovereign Soul

Now, gently bring your awareness back to your body.
Feel the weight of your hands, the rhythm of your breath,
the life pulsing in your veins.

You are here, in this moment,
as spirit made visible — the soul's art in motion.

When you open your eyes, let everything you see —
the light, the walls, the trees, the faces you meet —
remind you that Eden was never lost.
It is wherever you live in harmony with who you really are.

Take one more deep breath and say: "I am free. I am eternal. I am
home."

Open your eyes.
Smile.
Carry this remembrance with you into every choice,
every creation, and every act of courage that follows.

ABOUT THE AUTHOR

Vyana Reynolds is a visionary storyteller and regenerative systems designer whose work weaves myth, law, and ecology into a new story for humanity—one rooted in cooperation, sovereignty, and love for all life.

"Visionaries don't predict the future, they invent it!"

Vyana's life is a living myth, shaped by gentle rebellion, resilience, and radical reinvention. Again and again, she's broken through limiting beliefs to create a life that encourages <u>freedom and prosperity for all</u>.

At age 3, she faced food and financial insecurity—so she became an entrepreneur.

At 5, bored in kindergarten, she taught everyone long-division.

At 10, denied the right to play football with boys, she later became captain of her college's women's intercollegiate football team.

At 19, during a year abroad in Istanbul, she witnessed the oppression of women—so she became both an attorney and a self-defense instructor.

At 22, she overcame her greatest fear (sharks), when she learned to SCUBA dive in the cold and dark Salish Sea near her hometown of Tacoma, Washington.

By 28, she was writing non-profit legislation for Congress and winning a national award for her activism (empowering employees on Capital Hill). That's when she realized that *real* change doesn't trickle down from power structures, it grows from the roots up.

At 30, she walked away from civil rights litigation and created her own law firm, built on empowerment and the radical idea that clients should feel cared for—not controlled.

Not knowing how to escape the box of apartment living in Oakland, she bought an old sailboat in the San Francisco Bay and lived aboard for a decade.

At 35, disillusioned by the empty promises of the "American Dream," she met her Faerie Godmother and stepped into the myth of the mermaid to reclaim the parts of herself she had long suppressed—her feminine.

When she couldn't find mystical attire to reflect this inner change, she opened a nonprofit goddess shop where women could walk in tired and stuck—and walk out mythically transformed. Although the store was eventually sold, she still offers "mythic makeovers" one-on-one.

As Vyana stepped more fully into her mermaid persona, she hosted an international mermaid convention hosting 33 mystical mermaids from around the world.

Now living on the Big Island of Hawaii, Vyana swims on the reef and writes children's books to help others dive into the wonder of nature and transformation through story and play.

"The future of humanity isn't something we wait for
— it's something we create, together." Vyana

www.ingramcontent.com/pod-product-compliance
Lightning Source LLC
Chambersburg PA
CBHW070851280326
41934CB00008B/1397